Photographers
on
Photography

Photographers on Photography

Jerry C. LaPlante

A DRAKE PUBLICATION

STERLING
PUBLISHING CO., INC. NEW YORK

ACKNOWLEDGMENTS

I wish to acknowledge the assistance of Ms. Anna Winand at the International Center of Photography; Ms. Marjorie Neikrug of Neikrug Galleries, Inc.; and Mr. Donald Davidson.
Above everything, I wish to acknowledge the unselfish and extra-ordinary assistance of the photographers who make up this book. Their trust and candor was the key to everything.

Published by Sterling Publishing Co., Inc.
Two Park Avenue, New York, N.Y. 10016

Library of Congress Cataloging in Publication Data

LaPlante, Jerry C.
  Photographers on photography.

  1. Photographers—Interviews. 2. Photography.
I. Title.
TR147.L36   770'.92'2   78-7063
ISBN 0-8473-1764-1 pbk.

Printed in the United States of America

DEDICATION

I wish to dedicate this book, with much love, to Ted Mark Gott-fried. His encouragement has been limitless.

CONTENTS

Photo insert appears following page 32.

Introduction

This book is not a technical treatise designed to teach anyone about photography. There are many books on the market for that purpose. There is, however, a considerable amount of technical knowledge and opinion to be found in these interviews. It isn't possible to talk to anyone about their craft or art without such matters coming under discussion.

There is far more to photography, however, than f stops and exposure times, than cameras and films. The purpose of this book is to look behind the techniques and explore the people using them. One of the frustrations of putting these interviews on paper is the vast difference between the printed word and the picture. If I had my way, each reply would be accompanied by a photograph of the face of the person as he or she replied. Only then could the humor of Eva Rubinstein, Jay Maisel, Ruth Orkin, or Donald Strayer be appreciated completely. The understanding of Philippe Halsman or Phillip Harrington might be more visible. The energy and drive of James Cavanaugh, Lance Jeffrey, and Fred Mullane are vibrant in their faces as they speak. A peacefulness and love of their world shows in the eyes of Jack Dressler and Jim Wallace, at opposite ends of the photographic spectrum and years apart in age. Burt Glinn and Bill Stettner exude a professional confidence that I only hope comes across as strongly on paper as it does visually.

A filmed interview might satisfy the requirements of presenting a more complete image, but it does not allow the viewer the pleasure of going back and reviewing what was said. I found that I learned something more every time I went through each interview, from the original taping to the final editing. Only the written word allows this so easily. It must be pointed out that all the interviews were edited to some extent. Every effort was made to retain the full flavor and meaning of each subject's statements. I am a photographer myself, so I was as careful as possible not to intrude my own personality into the interviews themselves. If I have interfered anywhere with the communication between the photographers and the reader, I apologize.

It has been suggested that photographers may choose to photograph because of a need to communicate that they find difficult to satisfy verbally. In fact, this was articulated by Phil Harrington. "Articulated". is precisely the correct word. Mr. Harrington is a very well-spoken man. Perhaps I am lucky in my choice of photographers; I found each of them to be highly articulate. I do not know if this is a general characteristic of the successful photographer or not. My sampling certainly supports the idea. I would like to think that they each have a great deal to say to us and that they have found a satisfying medium in which to do it.

If there is one theme that appears throughout the interviews, it is that success in photography does not come from desire or talent alone. It comes from hard work and considerable sensitivity. Mostly it comes from hard work. I think something can be learned from the words of these photographers, whether you are a once-in-a-while snap shooter, an aspiring photographer, or a professional. Some of it is practical, some humorous, some just interesting, and some quite profound.

In this book photographers look at themselves and their craft or art. There seems to be much debate on whether or not photography is an art. In my opinion, the work of all the people in this book is art. Not all of them would agree with me. If your soul shows in what you do, it is art. These photographers have shown their souls in their work.

I hope the reader derives as much pleasure reading this book as I did compiling it. If it is only half as much, I will be well satisfied.

James
Cavanaugh

The business of photography continues to change. Older photographers have had to learn to adapt to changing markets, which they have done with varying degrees of success. A name made in one field of photographic endeavor will often open the door to other fields. But what about the young photographer starting out in today's enormously competitive marketplace without benefit of a previous reputation?

James Cavanaugh has been in business for only three years. He is making it. Perhaps his success can be ascribed to a combination of high technical skill and knowledge plus a decidedly good photographic eye. I am more inclined to think that both of these attributes came from his hard work and exceptional drive, and are only enhanced by the same. Skill and knowledge are not inherent characteristics. A good eye is kept sharp only by continual honing. Twenty-four-year-old Mr. Cavanaugh learns and hones, and produces beautifully, in and out of his studio in Buffalo, New York.

How did you get started in photography?

I started seven years ago as a hobby. I became very interested in it. I immediately, within about two or three months, found myself selling photographs to friends. At the time I was studying electrical engineering. I got on the yearbook staff, and that was the first time I was ever given assignments for photographic things.

Rather than deal with the yearbook people, I found it was much more profitable to begin immediately selling the pictures for the yearbook. I thought this was tremendous. I could be doing something I enjoyed, something that was creative, and I could make money at it. I decided to go to school at the New England School of Photography, which was about 50 percent arts and crafts school, 50 percent technical school. I went through two years of courses in a year and a half. When I came back to Buffalo I started banging on doors. I tried to get a position as an apprentice in a commercial studio, but at that time the unemployment rate here was over 12 percent, the economy was very bad, and I got the same story at every studio. "We used to have five people, but we laid them off, and I brought my wife in. Things are real tight right now." Finally, I found one large commercial studio that was doing well, and the photographer took me in as a summer replacement for his people as they went on vacation. I worked for several months with him, changing jobs all the time, as different personnel left on vacation. That was very beneficial.

I then decided to do it on my own. That's when I started going through the advertising agencies and such. I thought it was tough getting turndowns from the studios, but the ad agencies were even worse. The stories they came up with were beyond belief. At that particular point, I found the place I'm in now, which is fairly well located, with a very big ethnic population that's geared toward weddings. I figured, we'll give it a shot at that. The last year or so it's been very, very beneficial. It's been a growing business, and every month we set new records as far as sales. Still, my heart is in commercial photography and I'm working on a new portfolio now, basically studio shots. That's the goal right now, although we are continuing the portrait and wedding business because that is growing and it is healthy. We're just going to expand it. I'm bringing people in to help on the basic business.

Do you enjoy wedding and portrait work?

Well, the wedding work is a love-hate relationship. It's very tough to be creative when you're working on such a tight timetable. Unfortunately, a lot of weddings have a tendency to become very similar. It would be very easy to become bored and get plastic. The thing that keeps me going is that we try to do two or three new things with every wedding that we have never done before. This comes from talking to other photographers, attending conventions, seeing things, anything at all, something that strikes me as being interesting. We'll give it a try and see if we can change the wedding that little bit.

I think it is absolutely tremendous creative training, as far as pressure goes—knowing the equipment, working under a deadline.

In the long run, considering the number of hours involved, it's probably the least profitable thing that we do. It's one of our higher dollar sales, but again . . . We figure twenty-five or thirty hours work in each wedding. That's where the hate comes in.

It is very interesting to work under new circumstances. We try to use a great variety of equipment, rather than going in with one camera and one flash and saying, "Here, we're wedding photographers." We work with about 140 pounds of equipment at a wedding. Most of my colleagues doing weddings think I'm crazy for carrying all that gear around. But it seems to pay off.

What kind of equipment do you work with?

In the wedding end, 2¼ x 2¾, or 6 x 7 cm., cameras. Wide-angle, normal, and telephoto lens. We use multiple portable flash. That is also something a lot of my colleagues think I am crazy for. Rather than going with one flash on the camera, we try to use multiple lighting as much as possible. Here again, it takes a little bit more of my time, having to get the lights set up, but the results are better. More modeling, a much more full-looking photograph. Not harsh. I think this is one of the biggest things selling our wedding photography.

The portrait photography is just beginning to grow. It has seasonal peaks, especially at Christmas. I do enjoy that because I feel there are a lot of creative things you can do. We're trying more and more environmental . . . and there again, every time somebody comes in, their particular features, what they want to portray, gives us a whole new set of problems, and we have to work around that.

We do some portrait photography that is more on a production-line basis. This is in regard to sororities and such. We have a great number of girls coming in in a limited amount of time. We take three or four photographs of each. But what we are going for is a certain style of photograph and we want a pretty smile. We don't have to strive for high creativity. We want consistency and a good expression. In portrait photography a good expression sells more than anything else. We can have the world's finest technique, but if the expression isn't there or the person looks unnatural, it's not going to sell. That can be borne out by a lot of photographers who are very poor technically, but get tremendous photographs, tremendous shots, tremendous images. They sell well, because that's what people are after.

We are getting into other things. Passport photography, other instant photography. This is more on the business end. There is less craft, less creativity involved. This is egg money, to let the other things grow.

Why did you go into this business, since it is such a competitive one? Or maybe it's not so competitive here.

Oh, it's incredibly competitive. In some ways that's very exciting. We try a lot of different things and we brainstorm a lot, and I get obscene phone calls on my answering machine from other photographers. At conventions photographers tell me, "That's never going to work. That's nuts." In some cases they have been correct. Things have fallen flat on their faces. When I think of the advertising dollars we have spent, I want to cry. But other things have worked out very, very well. I think in this case the more things that we try, the more our name gets out, the more people see our photography and hear about us, the better things will be.

The other reason I got into it was that I wanted to work for myself. I wanted to be my own boss. I enjoy the ability to be up very early in the morning, or to stay up very late at night and do my own work. And just being creative. Turning something out. I guess I could have started a hardware store or something else, but it doesn't have the creative aspects.

Another thing: When people tell me something in photography, show me a technique, I seem to retain it. This is not true with other things, other studies. I think it might have a lot to do with my very strong interest. I have tried to turn this around, and in the last two years I've been teaching photography on a free-lance basis. I lecture at a number of the local camera clubs here in western New York and southern Ontario and such. And that's very nice. It means getting to meet with other photographers and talking about photography. I give them my point of view, show them my techniques, and in turn I learn a lot from them.

How did you decide to do your training formally, at a school, rather than apprenticeshipping?

I think the thing that made me decide to go that route was that I just by chance met a friend of mine who was running a course, an expanded version of the Nikon school. I began to see how much my photography would improve, by leaps and bounds, by having people instruct me on technique. Not necessarily visual things, but on proper exposure, proper handling of materials, the proper piece of equipment to use for the proper assignment. The work improved immediately. It was a quantum leap. I figured if I could have this out of a ten-week course, if I took intensive technical training for two years, it would have to be an even more tremendous leap. Looking at the schools, I ruled out any of the schools on a traditional basis, like R.I.T. (Rochester Institute of Technology), and went more for a vocational, technical school, where I would get complete emphasis on photography. Not sociology, not mathematics, nothing on that line. I think it was very, very helpful.

Would you go the same route again?

Yes. I would go to a different school though. I would find a school that is more on a business basis. I think photography has been glamorized. If I can spend 5 percent of my working hours during the day behind a camera making photographs, that's a lot. Most of the rest is business forms, dealing with people, returning files, filling out my taxes, paying my bills, soliciting work, working on advertising, working on new ideas to bring the business in. Today I did no shooting. I did a lot of work printing. I did a lot of processing, finishing prints, framing, and such. I made no images. I think this is the thing a lot of people have to understand. All the rest of this has to go along with it. It is something that is misunderstood by a lot of people who want to be photographers.

I also research a photograph. A portrait. Do you want it for a husband, lover, boyfriend, girl friend, or do you want it for Mom back in Wisconsin? Or do you want a business portrait? Each one has a whole different aura. On a wedding, we spend three or four hours of research time, which we call consultations, just talking with them. Sitting, letting them tell us exactly what they want. Telling us about their wedding, giving us ideas that they have.

In commercial photography, the research is even greater. On a recent album cover I did, we had to talk about the entire concept, what kind of mood they wanted to portray, and then what the technical requirements were, with the printer and such. In that particular case, that was three to four hours of research. The shooting session took fifteen minutes.

You are now doing all your own processing. Why?

One good reason: There is one superb color lab here in the city. I don't think there is anybody better, anywhere. However, for a 16 x 20 color portrait, they charge me $15 more than I charge my customers.

Working again with an outside color lab, especially in Ektacolor, a transparency is not such a problem as long as they keep their line in order—but when working with Ektacolor there are so many variables that quality is a problem. For a while we had a lab that did a good job. Then all of a sudden quality went down the drain. So I have arranged with another photographer to share darkroom space, and the quality is much better. I can print exactly what I want. I can crop to my customers' specifications.

Do you enjoy doing your own printing?

Yes and no. Again, it is a love-hate relationship. I enjoy doing it. I enjoy trying new things and being in control of the print from the beginning to the end. The only problem is the time factor. It does eat up a lot of time. We have mechanized equipment. It's not done by hand. But, again, it takes my time. I could be doing other things. If the volume becomes high enough, I will hire somebody to do it. Then, at least, I'll be dealing with one of my own employees and I can let him know exactly what I want.

It's also a selling point. People are becoming much more sophisticated about what they buy. Before, you could have it done in a lab and people really didn't know the difference. But one of the questions they are starting to ask is, "Do you do your own processing or do you have it sent out?" And having it sent out is sort of a derogatory mark.

The other thing that this opens up is that if somebody needs something very quickly, we can produce it. If I were still using an outside lab it couldn't be done, or it would be done only at a much, much higher price.

Do you do any shooting for your own pleasure?

Sure. A number of times I've gotten so involved with what I've been doing that I sold off my 35mm cameras to purchase other equipment that was necessary for the studio, because I don't use 35mms for commercial or job purposes that often. I figured that I know enough people I could borrow one from if I needed it. And as soon as they were gone I had to have them back, just to shoot on my own.

I think that's the most fabulous thing—the learning experience—just putting film through the camera. You go back over your transparencies or contact sheets and try to understand why you took each individual photograph. Obviously something made you push the shutter button. You look at the picture and say "Why" and "How can I fine-tune this?" That's the most tremendous learning experience.

It's also very relaxing. I try to explore everything, from my wide-angle lens through the macro. On other days I get in a different kind of mood, and I take my view camera out and become an avid practitioner of the zone system. I will go somewhere with the view camera and one lens, and to make sure that I am very careful, I take about four sheets of film for the entire day's shooting.

It still awes me. It has a very strong interest, just to work on my own. I find when I begin to feel pressured here, on the business end, all I have to do is go out for a day and shoot on my own and produce nice things, and it makes photography all worthwhile again.

Do you ever sell the pictures you shoot on your own?

More and more I'm starting to. About a year and a half ago, I decided that when it is necessary to give a gift to relatives or acquaintances, I would give what I produce: photography. More and more people are beginning to look at these prints and decide they would like something like that for their home or office. It's becoming profitable at that end. That's also rewarding. To sell something that I really like. We are starting to display 30 x 40 prints in the studio, just to show people photographic art, along with our portrait and wedding work.

Another thing that is happening: In portrait photography, the first thing people still say here is, "How much is an 8 x 10?" When we try to suggest a 16 x 20 or 20 x 24 to them, they immediately feel it is very vain to put something like that on the wall, when indeed it is not. Years ago, people would have portraits painted, and they would be tremendous in size. We are trying to get people to see that this is something that should be in their homes. It can become part of the family heritage.

Do you invest in a lot of new equipment as it comes out?

I'm not tremendously equipment crazy. I don't rush out to get each new gadget. A friend of mine says something that I think is absolutely true, and that is that you can judge the amount of a photographer's frustration by the amount of equipment he has. Again, I carry a lot of equipment to weddings so I have the possibilities, but 80 percent of my work is done with one body and a normal lens. It also facilitates me knowing what I am doing.

For my studio portraits, I use a banged up old Mamaya C330 with a 135mm lens. It works well. I know the camera, I know what to expect out of it. In 35mm, I use Olympus. It does the same job for me that my Nikons did. The lenses seem to function just as well. The 30 x 40s I have had made from them are gorgeous. And it's a lot less expensive. I used to have a lot of motor drives and a lot of fancy equipment. I found it wasn't doing anything for me.

I would much rather spend the money a motor drive would cost for several different sets of optics so I can have different visual effects, rather than be able to shoot fast.

It is obvious from your work that you are a highly skilled technician as well as a creative photographer. Apparently your training was put to good use.

I believe in this very, very firmly, and the classes I teach are geared toward this. If you have a great visual eye, that's one thing, but if you cannot produce a technically good print, you're wasting everything that's there. I think people should study the technical end first.

What burns me most at camera clubs are the people who come out and say, "Ha, this got six stops underexposure, and this one got six stops over-exposure, and I got the pictures." Great, if you want a technically poor print. I maintain that film has absolutely no latitude whatever. You have to get a basic minimum exposure, and you have to get an optimum exposure, to get the best technical quality.

Also, when I am printing, I don't need negatives that call for radical changes in print exposure and filtration for every print that I do. I need consistency so that I can work quickly.

I still have tons and tons to learn. I think that's the greatest thing. Things continually change. A lot of photographers don't want to learn. This is the biggest problem I have looking for wedding photographers. Poor technique.

What is your exposure system?

It's an incident system based on the zone system. We measure the light source, not the reflectivity. I think the best example of this is if somebody is using a built-in meter to photograph a race—if a white car goes by they zoom their aperture ring way down to f 16. A black car comes along and they open up to f 5.6.

Exposure is actually based on sunlight, and the sun is 93 million miles away. Now based on an inverse square, the earth would have to be knocked out of orbit 35 million miles to lose one stop of light. These people are constantly changing their aperture, but the sunlight is not changing. Then they can't understand why they have washed-out colors or very underexposed transparencies and such. We try to get them over to an incident meter, measuring the light, and when they do, all of a sudden things improve. You have to work out a series of tests for basic acceptable density when you are working with a negative material, and we have to program each person's meter on their equipment, their film, their paper. Because it will vary. This is just a brief statement on the system we are using. It works great. We can shoot under many different lighting conditions and come up with negatives that print an 8 x 10 at f 11 for eight seconds on Polycontrast Rapid paper, every time. It may not be a fine-tuned print, but it is always a good work print. That's the kind of consistency I need, so that I can show people something quickly, with a minimum amount of time in the darkroom.

If you were conducting this interview, what questions would you ask yourself that I haven't?

I question myself a lot. I guess the most important thing is, "What am I going to be doing tomorrow? What new things can I try?" I think that's the most difficult thing for me. I tend not to be a self-starter, and I really have to give myself a kick in the butt. I'm always trying to find new things to do. In the business end, too, because I have to pay my bills. To do that I have to sell photographs. So I question myself. Once in while when things get a little tough, I ask myself, "Why am I doing this?" But that's generally not a hard question to answer. I enjoy it so much.

The other thing that I always try to do is critique myself on the work that I have done. I read something that I think is a great statement: " I'm only as good as the last photograph I produced." I've really tried to use that on anything I've done recently. I think the most important thing is to really work hard. The results are then the best.

Another thing: A lot of people think they are photographers simply because they take photographs. You're not a photographer until you have finished the cycle and you show your work. Showing your work can be selling your work to a customer, having it published, or just showing it to your family and friends and getting some type of feedback. It's good getting the feedback, finding out what other people think. I think that's important.

Jack Dressler

Magazine and billboard advertising is very visible. High prices are paid for the photography involved because the images are few and special. Yet there are areas within advertising photography that most of us take for granted. Consider the catalog photographer. He is seldom recognized because the objects he photographs appear mundane and his pictures are seen by only a few people: the buyers for large and small stores all over the country. Many of the items that stock their shelves have been purchased from photographs sent out by the manufacturer or distributor that were shot by the catalog photographer.

Jack Dressler has made his living for thirty years shooting these photographs, most of them in his studio in New York City. He does not look for awards for his work. He is, in a sense, a businessman who delivers a product—in the form of photographic prints.

Mr. Dressler is now sixty-three years old. He is self-taught, and he turns out work that is often much more esthetically appealing than the subjects he is shooting. He also sells to an entirely different market than do most of the photographers in this book. He has some interesting things to say about that market, as well as about photography.

How do you feel about your business?

Photography. It really is esthetic. But the trouble is, when you get into the business end of it, you know, even though it is esthetic, it loses its shine. You know what I mean?

I believe I do.

It loses a lot of its texture because of the discipline, because of rushing, the whole combination of its economics. People paying bills, not paying on time, not paying at all. It seems like the graphic arts industry is the last on any list to be paid. In many cases your customers go out of business. A lot of manufacturers speculate. They speculate on an item or a business, and it's short-lived. They just form a Chapter 11 and find another business. Those are the bad parts. The good part is that it's always something different. No two photographs are really ever alike. No two subjects are alike. These are challenges which are good. Because not many businesses have continuous day-in and day-out challenges. They do the same things, and after a while it becomes boring.

Is most of your work done for catalogs?

Yes. We don't do high fashion, bar mitzvahs, weddings. Sometimes we'll do people's photographs for publicity, but that's mostly as a favor for a company. But we try to stay away from it. We just concentrate on catalog advertising. People who manufacture or import new items, create new items, have to have a photograph so they can put it in a weekly or a newspaper, or a magazine, or they mail out the photographs themselves, directly, to the department stores. Most of these photographs are done about a year in advance. Let's say there are approximately a hundred different items. They aren't all going to be on the company shelves. They can't manufacture the hundred because there's quite an overhead. So they test it out with the buyers to see what the buyers like and don't like. What they like, they accept, and what they don't like they delete. and this way, they have a pretty good idea of what is going to be in demand, so they go into manufacuring and ordering. Lately, the way things are with imports, some companies can't come through on their orders. They get the orders, but they can't come through. This is the combination of headaches that feeds down to my business and determines whether I get paid or not.

Is most of your work done here? Do you ever have to go out and shoot large items?

Yes, we do location work occasionally with large items. Also publicity work, where people are receiving awards. Or machine plants that have precision tooling or manufacturing. But most of the work is toys, gifts, housewares, appliances, electronic equipment, a whole combination of things like that.

Do you carry the procedure all the way through, doing the photographs and the layouts?

In most cases the layout is left to us, because we know it through experience. Occasionally, an advertising agency will bring in stuff and suggest what layout they want. Unless we feel that they are wrong, we go along with them. They know their business, but we know what a lens can do. They see something with their eyes, while I see something how the lens is going to see it. I may advise a change in the perspective, for instance. The guy says, "I want it my way." At least I've told him. So, afterwards, if something looks wrong, they don't say to me "Why didn't you tell me?" I have to protect myself sometimes by making these suggestions. And I'm not always right. Everybody's human. But at least we try to do the best we can. There are a lot of good photographers. The thing about photography is the service, getting the work out on time, because no matter what, if you delay an order and things don't get sent out on time, and if it is too late, it could kill a whole season, a whole idea. Photographs have to reach the clientele as quick as possible, so they can see the new items. Everything is competitive. Everybody is making the same item. They say they're not, but they really are. The labels are a little different, but the ideas aren't.

So the photograph that you take may very well determine whether that particular customer sells over a competitor?

You bet. We took photographs of a few dolls not long ago, and the customer just mailed them out, and he told me he got a $50,000 order just from the photograph itself. Sometimes the photograph can make a dollar item look like a $10 item, and sometimes it can make a $10 item look like a dollar item. We used to photograph a lot of Spode and Wedgewood, and they didn't come out as good as some of those Japanese plates that came in. What the texture reason is, is hard to explain. But sometimes we would have trouble with the contents of the plates or the depth of the plates, or the coloring or whatever. Light greens and light yellows are difficult to pick up in black and white. Color is something else.

Most companies are very competitive. They all manufacture pretty much the same items, even though the import people say that you are getting the only item of its kind. They tell each importer they are getting an exclusive. Not so.

Another thing about my photography that is becoming difficult is that most of our imports used to be from Europe. When they came to America, we did the photography here. Importations came from Europe to the United States, from Czechoslovakia, Italy, France, etc., and we did the great bulk of the photography. What's happening now, because of the competitive prices, is that the Far East, Taiwan, Formosa are now doing the manufacturing and exporting. And they're doing the photography over there, too. Packaging, the artwork. And they are getting it done far cheaper, which has hurt, hurt tremendously the graphic arts field, because it's being done elsewhere.

How tough is the competitive situation here?

Well, there are a million photographers. And each one has his locality. but a lot of photographers work directly with advertising, strictly advertising agencies, where there are budgets, mark-ups, etc. My business is primarily with the manufacturer and the importer. A few agencies. The trouble sometimes with the agencies is that they have ideas, they tell you what to do. You do it. You spend a lot of time. Ane then you do it over. And you don't get paid for it because what they think and what has to happen are two different things. The manufacturer is only concerned with getting good photographic prints. You get more money from the advertiser because of the budget. But you get a whole lot more work done with the manufacturer.

About the price of photographs. We are a little higher priced than most of the field. The reason is, either you make a living or you don't. Otherwise you work day and night in this business just to meet your overhead. But we can make ten photographs and charge, let's say, $25 each where another company charges $15. The thing is this: We'll do it in two hours and it will take them a whole day. So we are still ahead of the game. They make a big production and demonstrate the temperament of photography. We don't make any production. We just make the pictures.

Our lighting system here is not like some studios that have spaghetti all over the floor. We have a system of lighting that uses less electricity, concentrating lighting like an artist uses a brush, for the highlights and the dark areas. It is hard to describe. It really has to be shown. Even with the best we can do to keep costs down, business goes down. A lot of the companies have just faded away, gone out of business. One of our companies that used to do $50,000 a year went out of business. Another company moved down to North Carolina, so I mean this business has had various changes.

Has your own business maintained?

My business has fallen down a lot, only because my big accounts have just disappeared, like I just described. And there's nothing much you can do. Getting new business . . . most people will give you the business if your price is less than they are paying, and this I'm not about to do, because I don't want to knock myself out and make very little profit. It doesn't pay. I'd just as soon go out of business and do free-lancing. Make it my own way, without all the overhead.

I know painting is your avocation, and some of your work is most impressive. You have been doing it for years. Did you ever do any photography for the fun of it?

I used to do a lot of it, many years ago, for the fun of it. The creativity, the beauty, the lighting. Like the other day, I wished I had my camera with me. I was playing golf, and the sun was at a six o'clock low, and the green was yellowish green, and the long shadows, and the Throgs Neck Bridge in the background. It was a tremendous, beautiful photograph. But I didn't have a camera with me. But the most important part about this is not so much taking the picture, but recognizing it and seeing it, which I enjoy. Most people never see beauty, they just pass it by. This is a fact. Most people pass by the beautiful things in front of them. I don't. There are an awful lot of those things. When I travel, I do the same thing.

Tell me a bit about the equipment you use.

Most of our work is done with an 8 x 10 camera. We don't do any blowups. We don't have any time for blowups. We shoot with 8 x 10 film, and the reason we do that is that a lot of customers want fifty prints or a hundred prints, and to blow them up takes a long time and it's much more expensive. So we are equipped with automation and we turn out 8 x 10 contacts quite fast. The color we farm out. We do a lot of work in color, but we farm out the print-making. It doesn't pay to make color prints.

When you work with color, do you work with negative or reversal film?

Anything. We shoot a lot of transparencies. We shoot a lot of color negatives, to make color prints. We do a lot of catalog work with transparencies. Sometimes we shoot 35mm in color for people who want to project and talk about their subjects. You know, it's a funny thing about business. Sometimes you get a lot of one thing in a week, and you'll find that most of the stores are doing the same thing. And that's why this is all being done. Then all of a sudden you're making 4 x 5 black and whites, which you hardly ever do. It's Sears, that demands 4 x 5 prints, but it just comes out throughout the year, once or twice. The rest of it is 8 x 10, black and white, or color, contacts and color prints.

Would you recommend this particular field of photography to a young photographer just starting out?

Well, I wouldn't say, because I'm not that young anymore. Someone with more energy, who is young, probably could make a go of it, but it all depends on the individual. The worst thing I ever did was make a studio. I should have free-lanced from the very beginning. I would have made less but I wouldn't have that overhead and headaches and all that. It would have left me time to travel and do my art work. But you get caught up in this, because customers need this and customers need that, and you can't get free.

Burt
Glinn

Burt Glinn is one of a small group of highly creative photojournalists who turned their journalistic talents to the industrial world after the demise of the big picture magazines. He has done this with considerable success. He is also anticipating, and participating in, the possibilities inherent in the return of picture magazines.

Mr. Glinn has photographed for the annual reports of Pepsico, Olin, Pfizer, General Motors, Inland Steel, Richardson-Merrell, Damon, Xerox, AMF, Revlon, Bristol-Myers, Northeast Utilities, CONDEC, Consolidated Can, Alcoa, and many others. He has photographed industrial books for IBM and Kwasha Lipton.

His advertising clients include IBM, TWA, The House of Seagram, BOAC, Chase Manhattan Bank, the Government of Puerto Rico, Sabena, Geigy Chemical, ITT, ESSO, Sea & Ski, Dry Dock Savings Bank, and Gulf and Western.

He first came to public attention for his superb photographic coverage, in color, of the South Seas, Japan, Russia, Mexico, and California, for Holiday magazine. Each locale was given a complete issue, a demonstration of editorial confidence shown to few photographers.

In collaboration with author Laurens van der Post, he has produced two books: A Portrait of All the Russias and A Portrait of Japan. His recent editorial work has included stories about Los Angeles for Esquire magazine, the Metropolitan Opera for Fortune, Haiti and Great Cats of Kenya for Travel and Leisure. He has done reports on the Sinai War, the U.S. Marine invasion of Lebanon, Castro's takeover in Cuba, and both political conventions in 1976, as well as personality profiles of Sammy Davis, Jr. and the late

Senator Robert Kennedy, for magazines such as Life, Paris Match, and Newsweek.

Mr. Glinn holds the Dana Reed Award from Harvard University, the Matthew Brady Award as the Magazine Photographer of the Year from the University of Missouri and the Encyclopaedia Britannica, the Award for the Best Book of Photographic Reporting from Abroad from the Overseas Press Club, and the Gold Medal for the Best Print Ad of the Year from the Art Directors Club of New York.

Mr. Glinn comes from Pittsburgh and has been around for fifty-two years. He has served three terms as president of the Magnum Photographic Co-operative, of which he has been a member since the beginning of his career. He is the first Vice President of the American Society of Magazine Photographers.

When he isn't running around the country or the world, he resides in New York City.

Has your training always been in photography?

No, I have no photographic training.

You are strictly self-taught?

Well, when I was a kid, I got a camera as a present and I started taking pictures. I used to read books in the library on photography. I learned about the theory of color from a book about one-shot color cameras. I don't know if you remember, but before there was Kodachrome, and even after there was Kodachrome, they used to have what they called one-shot cameras. When they did commercial work, the small format wasn't considered acceptable. Even in the early days of the fifties when I was first working for Life magazine, they wouldn't deal with 35mm film. They thought they couldn't engrave it. For commercial work they used 4 x 5 cameras that had three separate film plates, a big, bulky camera. It had a beam splitter mirror that would split the light coming through the lens into three separate beams. They would have the three complementary color filters in front of the black and white film, and therefore they would shoot three separation negatives in the camera. It was like making a dye transfer print, but they made the separation negatives when they made the picture. I've never used one of those cameras, but I learned the theory of color, of why color photography works, at the age of fourteen or fifteen, by plowing through that book. It really explained something. If you understand how that camera works and why you get color from that, then you understand it technically.

So far, everybody I've talked to has not had any formal photographic training or taken any courses.

Well, I don't believe in them. I think there are some good people who have taken them, but as a rule. . . . When I travel, I try to call a school or something if I want somebody to help me. I use a professional assistant, but if I need a second assistant, it's always nice to call the kids from the schools. They show me their portfolios, and everybody who goes to the same school has the same kind of portfolio, which is a bad thing.

I think there are some marvelous photographic teachers. I don't know if they are good teachers for professional photography, in the commercial sense. If you are going to photograph for specific purposes, outside of just your own self-expression, if you are photographing for a client—and that goes all the way from photographing whiskey bottles for a whiskey manufacturer through doing journalism for a magazine—there are still requirements that are imposed upon you from outside, and that takes a certain degree of professionalism. Now, maybe photographic schools, some of the better ones, are good if somebody's going to do the kind of things that are hanging in galleries now, although I don't see much stuff hanging in galleries that I like. But I think the technical things of photography that have traditionally been taught in schools are things that people can learn. Now, I think that you can possibly learn them in a more concentrated way in a school, but you don't get any of the peripheral, fall-out things that you learn by working. It's unfortunate, but I guess there are so many people involved now in photography who want to get jobs as assistants. . . . I have a file a mile long of people applying for assistantships. But I found that was the best way to learn.

I think you get a narrow, limited education at a photographic school. I think that the technical skills of photography are something that can be learned in many ways. And not necessarily in school. I think the problem about going to a school of photography is that you don't get enough exposure to the other kinds of things that you should know—Greek, Latin, the social sciences or government, or American literature. It's more important, when you are young, to discover what you want to say, to get a background, a platform from which you can talk. Photography, even in its most abstract form, is some kind of communication. If you are a highly skilled technician in it and you have no cultural basis from which to make any statements, it's silly. You've talked to Philippe [Halsman]. Philippe is a marvelous, rounded, cultured gentleman. Most of the people you will talk to who are successful in photography are not shallow people.

I think you can get training in all kinds of things, and it depends on what your interests are. I am more interested in people who are more interested in life, what the world is about, what our culture is about and where we came from, than in people who are just interested in the technical aspects of photography.

Do you think the schools inhibit creativity rather than foster it?

Well, look. Some people are really talented and they are going to do it whether they go to school or they don't go to school, and I wouldn't want to make a generalization. Maybe schools work better for some people than for others, but by and large, if a young person came to me and said, "This is going to be my education," I'd say, "I think that's a limited education."

The picture that brought your name to my attention was the "Winter in Siberia" photo in the Time-Life Photography series. That is one of the most marvelous shots I have ever seen.

I think we're talking at a very interesting point for photographers, time-wise. I'm a member of Magnum [a group of photographers who organized in the 1930s to sell their photographs] and it's a full-time occupation just being involved with it. It's been like a sine wave, what has happened, how we get our money for taking photographs. We're professional, and most of us live off the money we make from photography. If you want to live well, you've got to do well. I came into photography in 1950 and I worked as an assistant for *Life* magazine, and that's where I got my training, really. Then, through the '50s into the early '60s, we could keep busy doing all kinds of marvelous things. In Magnum, we didn't even have to have assignments. We could do it and then sell it. That meant covering all kinds of news events, which were a delight to me. I liked doing them. I went to Havana when Castro came to power, and we covered Khrushchev traveling across the United States, and we did the Queen of England's tours, and I was in Israel for the '56 war. We did all those kinds of things, and it was a burgeoning market. Then somewhere in the middle of the '60s the magazines began to wither and die. We recognized this and we made an attempt to organize a new market, which was largely through the industrial world, and whatever was left of the editorial world. We've done very well financially through these industrial things. We probably do, as a group, more annual reports than anybody else, and we get some of the best ones. Now we are on the verge of an absolute explosion of editorial necessities again. There were 800 magazines last year that people invested some degree of money into, either investigating or starting them. Very few of them will have the kind of budgets that we used to have, the kind that would send you around the world.

That picture you talked about, the Russian, Siberia, picture, was done on assignment while I was doing Russia for *Holiday*. They kept me in Russia for three months. I was able to take two separate trips to the Soviet Union. They paid two air fares and I lived there for three months. I don't think there is going to be very much of that again, not even with *Life* coming back, although I suspect that *Life* is going to be an enormous success. But they're not going to have the kind of money they used to have. For their Great Cat series, they sent John Dominis to Africa for nine months. They're not going to have that kind of money. It's a different kind of market, but there is a great, great explosion of the necessities. Photographers can realize this and figure ways of financing their projects, and they will own their material—which is a theme that will run through everything I say, because I fought all my life never, never to give up the rights to the pictures. We sell and license only publication rights and we keep the pictures.

Photographers will find ways of going back. The artifacts on my walls here are from the Sepik River, in New Guinea. That was another *Holiday* project on which I spent two months in the South Pacific. Well, now we're going to find other ways of putting together trips and projects like that. There aren't going to be a lot of them. There will be some, but not a lot. If we do that, and are able to edit well—you've got to be a good editor, and get the story in good shape—then there will be demands in lots of ways. We have a growing amount of income from second sales. It is rather enormous now, and we have a library organized, and people are going to have to learn to do that. But doing that means you have to be more than just technically skilled. You've got to have the *idea* for the story. You're going to have to have a notion of what is important to say, or at least what is going to be read or looked at. And that takes more than just being a photographer.

Another thing is that the whole world is caught up in what I call "the emperor's got no clothes" syndrome. We made a cult out of a certain kind of fashion photography for a while, without much thought. I think we're coming to the end of it, but there was a cult of minimal photography. In order for it to be interesting, it had to be bad. The way to show that the world is banal is not by being banal yourself, but by being terribly perceptive and by saying something about the banality.

I just saw the Time-Life Yearbook on Photography for '77. Well, except for Jay Maisel's thing, everybody is just caught up in the museum world thing. I couldn't believe it.

This has become part of a whole market on its own. It has made so many photographers very self-conscious. If I shoot this, I will get myself hanging in the Museum of Modern Art.

Yes, well, you see, that's already crap. I think Szarkowski [John Szarkowski, the Director of Photography at the Museum of Modern Art in New York City] is an intelligent man, but I think he has much too much influence and controls much too much of the photographic part of the establishment. I don't want to politicize this thing, but it's silly. When something is crap, it's crap, and you say it. There are certain things that you've got to bring to a photograph, more than just your sense that the world is a banal place.

The world is not basically a banal place.

As a matter of fact, that is a contradiction of the basic premise of what I have found in photography.

I'd like to talk to you about corporate photography and annual report photography.

Well, it all comes to the same thing. I use the same mind and the same set of standards when I'm doing whatever I'm doing for some client. It really comes from the thing that I think I discovered by being with Magnum and being in journalism. It's that people who are critics and people who are museum directors always have to look for some kind of new technique or something. If you're going to have to write about something, you're going to have to write about different things. And photographers don't, necessarily. There is no way, if you are being genuinely photographic, that you are going to be repetitious, because the world keeps changing. Your perceptions keep changing. I never really thought it was a matter of using wide lenses or shooting from the middle of your belly or not looking in the viewfinder. These are all devices that are gimmicks, not photography.

We got into corporate photography because the magazine market was declining, was changing. And there was more money in corporate photography, which is kind of interesting to be involved in. I started slowly in it, and in the past years it's gotten to be rather important. I do maybe 100 or 150 days a year, at least, in corporate photography. What I try to bring to it is a kind of journalistic intelligence, analyzing what the problem is, what we are trying to say, what we're going to do. What is the message that the corporation wants to convey? You've got to make a decision early whether you are going to lend yourself to this or not. You may disapprove of what the corporation wants to say. You'd better decide that early, not in the middle of the game. What with the SEC [Securities and Exchange Commission] standards and everything, most corporations do a fairly decent job of honest presentation. They do exaggerate their contributions to the environment, and some of them exaggerate their minority-hiring devices.

The companies that I work for, by and large, are very good that way. Not that I chose them that way, but I find there is an honest effort in a lot of places to really bring minorities in. They are much more aware this year than they were last year, and last year than the year before. There are also more qualified minority people now. I did a lot of work in the past, not recently, for Chase Manhattan Bank. They had a very deliberate policy of trying to hire minority people, as many as they could, and they were hiring them in positions where mistakes could cause a great deal of problems. I saw many difficulties. If you feel discriminated against, you're liable to be overaggressive about seeing supposed slights, or even the kind of slights we all get as we work, and there are tensions. But they made a really good effort to do it. IBM has been incredible. I just did a recruiting brochure for them, and I had to be careful that it didn't look like we were setting it up as we walked through, because there were so many minority employees. They have the most qualified, most sophisticated minority people working for them that I have ever seen.

Are they hiring more women?

Yes. I see a lot of women. They do knock themselves out to display the woman engineer here, or the woman physicist. There are not a lot of Ph.D's working up at IBM's Yorktown Research Center who are women. One woman there happens to be quite attractive, so she is being photographed more than she is researching.

I've been doing more and more interesting kinds of reports. You get the usual ones too, of making the factory look good. It's hard work, it's not easy work.

Could you comment on the technical problems involved?

Different photographers approach them in different ways. I carry an enormous amount of equipment, and maybe I ought to reexamine that and do it differently. I use strobe lighting when I can, but in a very natural way. This makes it very hard in factories, because something with a very high ceiling and a dark ceiling can't be lit naturally. It just doesn't work. One man, who I think is brilliant in the industrial field, doesn't use anything but a 15-watt bulb now and then. Maisel, who is very, very good in the industrial field, doesn't carry a lot of equipment. He carries a lot of cameras, he carries a lot of film, but he doesn't do a lot of lighting.

I have a tendency now to do a lot of my shooting on Kodachrome. I almost never get off of Kodachrome. If I *have* to get things that are moving, and the lighting is bad, I will go to High Speed Ektachrome and push it. But I try to get almost everything on Kodachrome. I find a lot of pictures can be shot at half a second, a full second, and give a lot of impact, without even deliberately blurring things.

How do you solve the problems of mixed lighting—skylights, mercury vapor lamps, fluorescent lighting, incandescent fixtures all in one area?

I don't solve them. I always shoot so that it gets pinker rather than greener. I don't find incandescent lighting on daylight film, if it isn't the only lighting, unpleasant. On the other hand, I find daylight shooting on incandescent film very unpleasant. So if I go into a factory that has daylight coming in, and also has fluorescents, I will shoot on daylight film with a 30-magenta filter and let the daylight go pink. It's not as good as if it didn't go pink, but you can live with it. It's much better than if the daylight part is okay and everything else is terribly green. There are just certain things you have to deal with. You use your intelligence and let it go. If they want something that is a perfect reproduction of color, then we should start with a different supposition and they can't ask me to do ten pictures in a day, or do a plant in a day. I can do one picture in a day. I carry 4000 watt-seconds of strobes, but I could carry 10, 12, or 16 and do it. I learned how to use strobe lights from John Mealy. Then I learned from one of my assistants who had been a studio manager for Carl Fisher. Much later, I learned how to do a different kind of strobe lighting. Now, I can do it both ways—soft studio lighting and the dramatic lighting that Mealy used to have, with rim lighting and direct lighting and back lighting.

How much shooting do you do for your own pleasure?

We were talking about this yesterday. My life is very complicated. Because of the things I've done and said about photographers' rights and ownership, I'm really involved on the board of the ASMP and I may very well be on the executive committee in the next three years, and that takes time. I'm very involved in running Magnum. I have been president. Charlie Harbutt is president now. We spent two or three hours yesterday just talking about how much you shoot for your own pleasure. I'm a strange kind of guy. I'm a very pragmatic photographer and I just like taking pictures. So I get a great deal of pleasure out of doing almost everything. I'm going to Paris tonight. We're going to do a story for *Esquire* called "A Gentleman's Guide to Paris." Well, that's going to be fun. The editor is my friend, and he's going over, and Pierre Salinger is going to work with us over there. The first story that Pierre and I did together was on the Pendleton Roundup, in 1956. From Pendleton to Paris. That's fun for me. The best things that I've done, I've done on assignments that were loosely defined. In other words, working for Frank Zachary at *Holiday*—Frank is now the editor of *Town and Country*—but working for him at *Holiday*, for me, was almost like doing pictures for myself. I didn't get caught in the trap of having to do the society ladies sitting in front of the castle, and so forth. I used to do whole issues, and whole issues were on the kinds of subjects that I was interested in, which they gave me out of the kindness of their hearts. I did the islands of the South Pacific, I did Mexico, I did Japan, I did Russia. I didn't do the kind of set piece that *Holiday* did. Russia was the first one that I had as an entire issue and that is a hell of a gamble for a magazine, because they are always on deadline. When I came back from Russia that week, the magazine had to go to press and there was no time to do anything else. I guess they must have been a little nervous about it.

Do you generally do your own story work?

Well, on the *Holiday* things, the only instructions I had were, "Kid, I want you to go do some snaps of the Soviet Union," and he told me it was going to be the whole issue. They got very nervous on the first two special issues I did for them because I spent the first month just being there, absorbing it, organizing what I wanted to do and how I wanted to do it. Yeah, I try to be my own editor. I try to figure out what the requirement of the story is and how to shoot it. It got close to doing my own work when I had those things for *Holiday*, because the requirement was to probably try and define some vision of the Soviet Union, not political, and perhaps not social, but cultural. I chose who I would be photographing and what I would be photographing, and I just went ahead and did it. It turned out that the writer and I thought a lot alike about certain things, and it worked out very well. We didn't have any problems with it.

Now, somebody like Elliott Erwitt, who I think is a most brilliant photographer— he's also a best friend of mine— has a complete dichotomy between the things he does personally and the things he does professionally. That's because his talent is much deeper, perhaps. His personal vision is so special that magazine editors can't find a way to use most of his personal work, which is a crime. His book, *Photographs and Antiphotographs*, is a great book. Now you can't buy it anywhere. The idiot publishers got rid of the plates. It's nowhere.

It is interesting that Elliott is beginning to do very well by selling his black and white prints, as prints. He is certainly not in the new vogue of gallery photographers. He's a classic photographer, but God, there is such perception in his work and it makes such a very personal statement. One of the reasons that critics can't deal so easily with photographs is that unless they are describing something that is new, technically, or something that is new in visual organization, or something that doesn't really exist . . . they can't really describe in words the impact of why Erwitt's photographs are great.

Unless a photographer with a certain perception and vision encounters viewers with similar perception, it isn't transferable anyway.

Well, it isn't. But the thing is that if your perception is good enough, people pay attention to it, and certainly people, when they are exposed to Erwitt, see it. Now whether it will ever work for a mass market. . . . He certainly is a very successful industrial and advertising photographer, and magazine photographer . . . but he's best when he is cut loose. There is a real dichotomy between Elliott's personal work and his professional work. There isn't in mine because, perhaps, I'm not as good as Elliott, at the highest and deepest level. But technically, and for serving the purposes of clients, I do a very good job.

The other thing you have to understand in corporate photography— you're solving people's problems. Now some people who are really great photographers can be absentminded and lose their tickets, and get lost on the job, and call back to find out where they're supposed to be the day after, and that will work. If you are *very* good. But corporate people are corporate people, and they like to be confronted with somebody who has a certain amount of efficiency and intelligence in attacking the job and figuring out what their problem is and how we can do it, and how we can do it in the most convincing way. I have always brought my training as a journalist, and my belief that photography is the best when it is least controlled, to the corporate world. If I have to do people working, I would rather do them really working, rather than contriving an idea beforehand.

There are times, however, when a company says, "Well, we want to see our customers." Then you go into this terrible problem of having to set up people sitting listening to records or buying toilet paper or using underarm deodorant, and these are all rather stilted kinds of things. I try to do it in ways that are as real as possible. There are other people who construct kind of Norman Rockwell pictures. Reid Miles, out on the coast, is fabulous at that, but to me, that's kind of a joke . . . and it's not a report. I think that if you want Norman Rockwell paintings of people using all the different products, you get Norman Rockwell to do it. That's a very effective photographic device, but I couldn't direct it that way. I mean there's a great deal of imagination in it, but I couldn't do it. What I try to do is make it as free as possible within a given situation.

We did last year's Seagram's report, which shows people in all kinds of situations using the various things that the House of Seagram produces. We did cast these pictures, but I used real situations. We wanted a sales convention, where people obviously drink. We wanted to show a big outdoor party. We wanted to show a bar and a fancy restaurant with young people who were willing to experiment, so we did a Japanese restaurant. But we created all the situations and then let them go, you see. We did an Italian anniversary party where shooting was easy. Two hours of shooting. But it took weeks, finding the family that looked right, putting them together, and getting them into a restaurant that we could light and have a corner to ourselves. It looked very natural, there is no doubt about it. That comes from just an appreciation that as far as I am concerned, my resources for inventing pictures are more limited than my ability to recognize and discover pictures as a situation develops. Now we have to have some control, because we have to have releases and all that, but I think reality is a great asset . . . the greatest ally that the photographer has. You can't direct people nearly as complicatedly and as marvelously as they do things naturally. It must be very difficult to try to make a movie that way because you've got to sustain it for a minute, or thirty seconds, or ten seconds, but a photographer needs only 1/100 of a second.

Do you work to an art director's layout?

No, I try not to work to a layout. I find working to a layout *very* inhibiting. Somebody calls with an interesting job and we try and do what they need done, yes. But I try to convince them that the more freedom we have to function, the better. They can say, "We've got to have verticals, we have to have horizontals, whatever you do we need twelve pictures out of that plant." It's not my function to redo the design. I work with a lot of good designers. Sometimes they tend to overcategorize photographers. They say,

"This guy's good at indoors and this guy's good at outdoors." Sometimes they don't know what they are missing. But by and large, they pick you for the kinds of things that you have done for them, so you are usually doing things that you know how to do or that you are particularly adept at. Some of the reports that I have are really very exciting. I'm doing a report for a drug company on cancer research around the world. Well, I'm in charge, but I have to check with them about where I'm going or what I'm doing. That's an enormously expensive, complicated report. I've been up in Iran, on the border of Russia. I've been to Japan for them, to do what's happening in the world of cancer research. I have to check with them, but the basic outlines of what will come out, of what we will say, will come out of the photography rather than out of the writing. There is a big responsibility for me to put whatever journalistic skills I have to work.

I did a report for Bristol-Myers a couple of years ago on the story of how you produce antibiotics. As complicated as it was, that is child's play compared to trying to organize your thoughts about cancer research, which is like a guerrilla war that is going on on millions of fronts.

It must be a very exciting type of . . .

Yes, but it's an excellent assignment. None of it is going to be what I consider *great* photography. It's going to be very good investigative, explanatory photography. I'm trying to explain things. I think great photography is when the whole thing is out of your control, and you recognize the moment and you do it. I'm old-fashioned now, I guess, but I like Cartier-Bresson, I like most of the Magnum people. I like what Gene Smith did, and naturally I like Walker Evans. I find that is great photography. Me going into a lab in California, where Dr. Burns is actually operating on a DNA molecule, actually cutting, and explaining in a picture how it works, because of lasers and all that . . . it's going to make a fascinating, interesting picture. It ain't art! I hate confusing art and commerce.

Look at a Halsman portrait. I think that is art, that is great photography, and it's shot at pretty much the same level as you are talking about.

Yes. Well, Philippe is of a different tradition. I found Philippe an enchanting teacher and a marvelous man and I really enjoy his portraits. It's just that I have a different view. Everybody has to define it for themselves.

If you were interviewing Burt Glinn, what questions would you ask him?

I think the key problem I have always had is to reconcile the fact that I wanted to live well with the fact that I wanted to do well. But I've got to tell you. The corporate annual reports can be good or they can be bad. I have always felt that whatever I do, once I accept an assignment, once I make the decision to do it, it is incumbent upon me to bring a great deal of skill, a great deal of professionalism to it, and I want it to look as good as it can within the parameters. Sometimes we fail. Sometimes you just can't bring off a picture in an industrial situation. Sometimes there's complete lack of understanding between the designer, the photographer, and the client. There very rarely is a misunderstanding between the designer and the photographer, in my experience. But a lot of times the client really gets very unhappy with it. But I believe that when I do a job, and it is totally mine, I don't want to be embarrassed by it. There has to be a certain plateau of excellence, and once you start charging the kind of money that we charge for industrial reports, or for anything. . . . During the last month we have had a girl off and I have been doing editorial work at one-fifth the rate, but I wouldn't consider putting any less energy or effort into something, even if it is for a small magazine. It may be just for them but it's got my name on it.

James Cavanaugh, original in color.

Above: Chris Evert, by Fred Mullane, original in color.

Top, right: Lillian Carter, by Donald Strayer.

Below: Mary Engel (Ruth Orkin's daughter) with Bob Hope, by Ruth Orkin.

Albert Einstein. Photograph by Philippe Halsman. Copyright by Philippe Halsman.

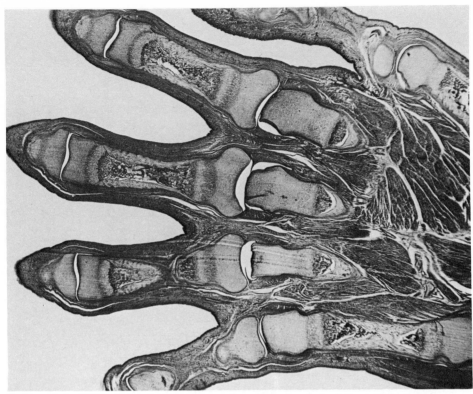

Photograph by Phillip A. Harrington. Cross section of the hand of a human fetus. Actual size, ½ inch.

Florida Forest, by Jay Maisel, original in color. Copyright by Jay Maisel.

D

Photograph by Lance Jeffrey.

Photograph by
Jim Wallace.

Below: "Nude on couch
with cushions," New
York, 1972, by Eva
Rubinstein.

F

Above: Illustration by Bill Stettner, for Columbia Records, original in color.

Below: Product photograph by Jack Dressler.

Xerox European Annual Report cover by Burt Glinn.

H

Philippe Halsman

Philippe Halsman was born in Riga, Latvia, in 1906. He studied engineering in Germany and then lived and worked as a photographer in Paris. Through the intervention of Professor Albert Einstein, he came to the United States in 1940 on an emergency visa and became a naturalized citizen in 1949. He now resides in New York City with his lovely wife of fifty-five years, Yvonne.

Mr. Halsman was the first president of the American Society of Magazine Photographers. Starting with his first Life cover in 1942, he ran a string of 101 covers for that magazine, as well as hundreds of other covers for both American and European publications—more than any other photographer anywhere.

In 1963 he received the Newhouse Citation, presented by the School of Journalism of Syracuse University. In 1965 he was one of three photographers representing the United States in the exhibit "Twelve International Photographers" in the New York Gallery of Modern Art. His work is represented in the permanent collections of numerous museums.

Two of his portraits, of Adlai Stevenson and Albert Einstein, were used on United States postage stamps. His portrait of André Gide was used on a stamp in France. In 1967 he was honored with the Golden Plate Award, presented by the American Academy of Achievement. In 1969, he was assigned by President-elect Richard Nixon to make his official picture.

Mr. Halsman has published six books: The Frenchman, the fairy tale Piccoli, Dali's Mustache, Jumpbook, Philippe Halsman on the Creation of Photographic Ideas, and Halsman Sight and Insight.

He is a master technician and his portraits are recorded with stunning clarity of detail. His prime goal and achievement, however, is the recording of the personality of each subject. At this he is a supreme master. He considers portraiture an exercise in psychological understanding more than in artistic composition. He achieves both superbly.

Have you done any other type of photography besides portrait work?

Yes. I worked for *Life* magazine as a portrait photographer for their covers, and I also made many independent journalistic stories for *Life*. They sent me, for instance, around the world to find and photograph the world's most beautiful girls. I visited sixteen different countries. For *Time* magazine I had to photograph the most beautiful queens and wives of presidents. I have photographed caverns and machinery for annual reports. I have published a book on Dali, a very surrealistic book. I have done practically all kinds of photography.

Is Dali a special friend of yours?

He is a special friend of mine. I have photographed him every year for the last thirty years.

I have photographed theatre, dancing, the Martha Graham group. There are very few things I have not done. For *Life* magazine I have even photographed landscapes—the southwest United States, Arizona, New Mexico.

You must prefer photographing people.

Definitely. I am mostly interested in people and so I prefer to photograph them. And photography put me in contact with the most important men and the most beautiful women of my lifetime. So it has made for a very interesting life.

I don't think anybody would object to traveling around the world photographing beautiful women.

Well, it sounds very pleasant. But, actually, it was a terrible rat race because I was given about four days in each country. I had deadlines to meet all the time, and the whole thing degenerated into a terrible rat race. Nevertheless, it was really pleasant and interesting, but, on the other hand, I lost something like fifteen pounds.

Was it worth the fifteen pound loss?

Well, eventually I gained them back. So. . . .

I remember the picture of Nixon leaping, in the back of *Life*. The book you did with everybody leaping in the air. Did that predate the picture of Dali leaping ["Dali Atomicus"] or did it come out later? In other words, was there any relationship between the Dali picture and the book?

No. No relationship. The idea came to me when I photographed the NBC comedians. NBC had more than two dozen different comedians working the television programs, and in order to advertise the shows the comedians were sent to my studio. I had two hours to produce one hundred or two hundred completely different pictures, showing them dancing, singing, mugging. And I also asked them to jump. Then one day a magazine asked me for photographs of a dozen different NBC comedians for an article. I selected the close-ups of their heads, and also their jumps. Suddenly, I realized that every one of them jumped in character. I became interested in the jump as an expression of the character of the jumper. If you are ambitious, your jump will be very ambitious. If you are passive and lethargic your jump will be very lethargic and unexciting. If you are an introvert, you will jump in a most unimpressive way. If you are an extrovert, you will probably make an interesting expression and you will spread your legs and your arms. So it was possible to read the character from the jump. That was one of the reasons. The other reason was to prove to myself that I had the courage to ask every important person that I photographed to jump. . . . And a third reason was to prove to myself that I had the power to make them jump. The Vice-President of the United States [Nixon was then Vice-President], or the Duke and Duchess of Windsor or Judge Learned Hand, whom I deeply respected, or Nobel Prize winners like Dr. Waxman or J. Robert Oppenheimer, and so on.

I think it is marvelous. You really predated the man who did the books on body language.

Yes. As a matter of fact, it is not impossible that he read my book and decided that you can interpret other body movements besides jumping. But the jump, in my opinion, is particularly interesting because it presents, for an adult at least, a completely unusual undertaking. He attacks it with the life-style that he has. His energy, imagination, and so on.

I read that when you do portraits you shoot relatively few pictures, that you feel all of the work should be done up in the head first. As a matter of fact, you have that marvelous self-portrait taken with your head resting on top of one of your tripods.

Yes. The idea was that the head of the photographer is more important than his camera. However, I do shoot, on the average, about twenty or thirty pictures during a portrait sitting, for the following reason: Usually a person is self-conscious, and it is my job during the sitting to help him overcome this self-consciousness. Very often, the more I shoot, the more the person forgets that he is being observed by the camera and the more relaxed and the more natural my sitter becomes. That is one of the reasons. The other reason is that I try to talk to him and cause an accident that will produce an interesting expression on the face of my subject. This you cannot do with only one picture. I prepare myself for a sitting by planning the lighting and the way I will photograph my subject. On the other hand, if I see that the subject does not correspond to my preconceived idea, I don't stick to it. And I try to photograph him the way he actually is and not the way I imagined him to be. That's only possible if you use a number of shots, and not decide that two or three shots will be sufficient.

In other words, you are not looking for the Philippe Halsman portrait but you are looking for the portrait of the person?

Yes. That's very true. I don't try to impress my own style on the subject. I try to get the subject to impress his own style on my photograph.

I try to photograph people with lighting that is three-dimensional. I try to make my picture photographically as sharp as possible. I go for the quintessence of the human being that I can capture in the photograph. Consequently, these three items do something in my photographs that makes people say they can always recognize whether it is my picture or somebody else's.

Your pictures are usually pretty obvious. Do you generally do a lot of homework on your subjects before you meet them?

Sometimes it is possible. If I photograph a writer, I try to read a couple of his books. But, very often, people that I photograph are practically unknown to me. I photograph a lot of presidents of great corporations for their personal publicity and for their annual reports. Usually I ask for a biographical sketch of the person I will be photographing. This also helps me to establish contact during the sitting because I consider that what you say to the subject is as important as what kind of camera you use.

Which brings up the question: What type of equipment do you use? At one time you designed, I understand, a 4 x 5 twin-lens camera for portrait use.

Yes. When I photographed the famous French writer, Gide, I photographed him with a view camera. He would take a very interesting pose. I would open the lens, set the focus, find an interesting composition, close the lens, put in my film holder, take off the slide, cock the shutter, and in the meantime the tension would be too great for the subject, and André Gide would completely have changed position and I would start all over again. So I realized that the moment somebody has an interesting expression, it was absolutely necessary to be able to shoot immediately, which was possible with the Leica or the Rolleiflex. But the format was too small and an 11 x 14 print was not as sharp and as realistic as the pictures that I made on the larger format.

Consequently, having studied engineering myself, I designed a twin-lens reflex that I could use with 4 x 5 negatives. However, in the last ten years I very often use the Hasselblad, which has marvelous lenses and is not as heavy as my camera.

Are you still very active? Still doing a lot of shooting?

I am not *very* active because I was much more active working for *Life* magazine. When *Life* magazine stopped I lost my best customer and also my display window. So I am photographing much less now but have found another very satisfactory occupation: I am teaching photography for the New School [of Social Research in New York City].

Do you think it is possible—you must because you teach—but do you think it is really possible to teach photography beyond teaching technique? Could you take an average person with average talent and develop him into an above-average photographer?

You see, during my many years at work as a photographer I learned many interesting things. For instance, that lighting can introduce emotional values. That the position of the camera can emphasize either the intelligence or the brutal strength of a face. That the inclination of the axis of the photograph changes the meaning of the photograph. All these things are not mentioned in books and are absolutely new to the young photographers I teach.

By the way, 80% of my class are professional photographers. So what it took me twenty, thirty, forty years to learn by trial and error and by analysis of my own and other pictures, is being taught the young person in a course that takes only thirty hours. Of course I cannot teach creativity, but I can teach technique. I can teach understanding of the photograph. I can explain to them what happens in the head of the subject while you photograph him. Since my course is called Psychological Portraiture, I am teaching not only photographic technique but also the psychological approach to portraiture. I usually hear from my students that this is the most valuable course they have ever had in photography.

I guess that answers my question. How long have you been teaching this course?

I think about six or seven years, for the New School. The course is over-subscribed and I am teaching two parallel courses and, as a matter of fact, I could also teach three parallel courses but I don't want to spend too much time in teaching because each session takes three hours and after three hours I am rather exhausted.

How many people do you have in a session?

Eighteen people.

How does one get into the course?

You have to present a portfolio of pictures to the head of the photographic department of the New School, and if you pass this examination of your portfolio and it is found that you are sufficiently progressed as a photographer, and if you do this ahead of the others, then you will be accepted.

So there is a certain sorting process, at least among these students. You are not going to get somebody in the course with no creativity at all.

Yes, there is a definite sorting process. Unfortunately, I do sometimes get people with no creativity. But I often have very gifted and talented classes. Sometimes there are classes that are very uninspired that make my job much more difficult than I would like.

The question of your own creativity is fascinating. You don't work in a style. A Philippe Halsman photo is generally recognizable, but there is never a style that follows through. There is always something different.

Somebody has described the style of an artist as "always plagiarizing oneself." So I don't try to make all my pictures after a certain fashion. I try to use as many interesting lightings as I can find, as many interesting positions. Monotony is one of the great enemies of creation, and I try to make my pictures as diversified as I can.

Are you generally happy with your results in that line? Or do you have times when . . .

Usually, the picture that I have in my mind before I take the portrait is much better than the picture that I eventually get in reality.

Does it ever work the other way?

No, very seldom. However, a few years later I forget what I expected to create myself and very often I am surprised at how good the picture actually is—the one that I didn't like in the beginning and that I considered to be a kind of disappointment.

Maybe you are less critical of yourself at that point.

Well, I am very critical of my own work and this is, in my opinion, a prerequisite of a photographer who wants to develop himself. If you think that everything you do is just marvelous, you will not improve.

I think that is a prerequisite for almost anybody in any field.

I agree with you.

Do you ever do any shooting strictly for your own pleasure?

Yes.

Have you always been able to do this, or have you found that work or commissions interfered?

No. I have taken some of my best pictures on commission. I am usually given sufficient freedom in solving a problem. If you look at these *Life* covers that I have made, each of them was designed not by an art director but by myself. On the other hand, if I find a face that interests me, I ask the person to pose for me. This happens, by the way, very seldom. Most of the pictures, 95 percent, that I made with Dali were made only for the pure pleasure of working with Dali and having such an interesting and amusing subject. Most of them were not published.

The mustache series that you did on Dali, and this one here ["Dali Atomicus"] . . . it is obvious that these were fun pictures.

Of course.

Have you ever worked as an art director, or along that line, with someone else doing the photo work at your direction?

No, I haven't done any art directing. But that means that I have never directed some other photographer by drawing a picture and telling him how to shoot a subject. But very often, before shooting a subject, I make a sketch of how I would compose my picture, and where, for instance, I would put the logo of the magazine.

If you were interviewing Philippe Halsman, are there any specific questions you would ask him?

I probably would ask, "What is the purpose of my photography, of my taking pictures?" What I am trying to capture in the picture is . . . I'm trying to sum up a personality as much as it is humanly possible. I know it is like the [mathematical constant] "pi." You never get the complete and final answer, but you can come as close to it as possible. It seems to me that if I am producing an honest psychological document about a human being, this picture might later become the visual symbol for the entire personality of my subject. In some cases it has worked out like this. For instance, my picture of Professor Einstein is now the picture that everybody thinks of when Einstein is mentioned. It was used on the postage stamp and it was used on the cover of many of his biographies. It is probably also one of the deepest and most interesting portraits that I have made.

I realize that a portrait sitting is actually a very artificial situation. I'm trying to combine the approach of the candid photographer with my approach in this studio or in the apartment of my subject. Unlike a candid photographer who has many days to be with his subject, I usually have only one hour or even less . . . or sometimes, when I am lucky, two hours. Therefore, I am trying to transform the artificial situation into the natural one. When I photographed Marian Anderson, I asked her to sing. When I photographed Marilyn Monroe, she didn't pose for my camera. She was flirting with the camera as if it were a human being. When I photographed Anna Magnani she was telling me about her son who was paralyzed by polio. So the sitting becomes not a confrontation of a camera and a human being, but a meeting of two human beings. I get, as a result, a photograph of a subject who is not posing in front of the camera but who is captured the way he actually is.

You speak of what you try to do with each subject. Would you use the same summation if you were talking about what you were trying to do with your entire life's work? As for your photo work, is there any pattern? Do you see any pattern or outline that you feel you are working within?

No, because from the very beginning I tried to make very realistic pictures and I am still trying to do the same. I'm also trying to shoot pictures which not only capture a human being but also convey some abstract idea. This is another part of my photography which is very important in my own eyes and for which, in the beginning, I was very often blamed. Many of these pictures were produced by special photographic techniques. *Life* magazine, especially, said, "Why are you doing these trick pictures?" They didn't understand that what I was trying to do was express an abstract idea in visual terms.

For instance, here is a picture on the cover of *Life* of Zsa Zsa Gabor with her ghost writer. When I photographed them, I put a gauze curtain between the writer and Zsa Zsa Gabor and because of that the ghost writer looks like a ghost. The words on the cover, which say "Zsa Zsa Gabor and Her Ghost Writer," are not only printed but also shown in the photograph.

Once I photographed a man who became a millionaire selling his hero sandwich. I photographed a giant hero sandwich in which he himself was the filling of the sandwich. That was, of course, a very interesting opening picture for the article on him. When I photographed the room of the Security Council of the United Nations, nobody was there. There was a big table, and I decided that something was missing in the picture. The condemned state that is lying as a victim on the table. I laid down on the table as though I were the victim myself, and asked my assistant to shoot the picture. And so I have a kind of prophetic picture of what the United Nations is doing to some of its members.

Where was that published?

It was only published in my own book, *Creation of Photographic Ideas*.

In most cases, a photographer is trying to produce as interesting a picture as he can. Most photographers forget that the onlooker, the viewer of the picture, has to have at least the same kind of sensitivity as the photographer. How often I have tried to capture the profound expression of a human being, and when I showed the picture to a photo amateur he would exclaim, "Isn't it amazing how you captured every hair and every pore in his face." But they don't see the most important thing: What I was after is the content of the picture and not the technique.

An article I recently read made the point that fashion photography has gotten a lot of press in the last few years. As a result, fashion photographers have become self-conscious and have lost sight of what they are trying to do with their photographs and instead are shooting their own egos.

In portrait photography you have a living subject, a personality which is the essence of what you want to reproduce. When you are dealing with a garment or a product, do you feel the same essence can be portrayed?

Well, I have done fashion photography myself for *Life* magazine, but eventually I tried to get out of it because when I did it, it was the most sterile kind of photography. The fashion magazines were mostly interested in garments and tried to produce beautiful pictures of dresses which were worn by beautiful women, but that was all. Eventually, fashion photographers became the avant-garde for progress in photography. Because they were always photographing the exterior, they were not interested in capturing the content. They were pushed, in order to make interesting pictures, to invent more interesting aspects of photographs. Consequently, the technique of photography and the unusual angles, the unusual lighting, the unusual views, were mostly developed by fashion photographers, who then produced a very important part of photography as we know it today.

I am interested in your feelings about "non-people" photography.

Well, you can produce a picture that is interesting because of its content, because of its depth. You can produce a picture that is interesting because of the way it looks. And the fashion photographers have produced many interesting photographs. This is as important as a photograph that has deep content. The word "photography" can be interpreted as "writing with light," or "drawing with light." Some photographers are producing beautiful photographs by drawing with light. Some other photographers are trying to tell something with their photographs. They are writing with light.

Usually, each picture tries to tell something. Sometimes—and this is the ideal—when it combines the form and the content, a picture that is telling something also has the look of a work of art.

Phillip A. Harrington

Phillip Harrington was born in Holland, Michigan. After graduating high school, he went to New York in 1940 and received his formal photographic training at the Clarence White School of Photography.

He spent the next six years doing newspaper work as a photographer for the Akron Beacon-Journal and the Miami Herald, as Director of Photography for the Wisconsin State Journal, and as Acting Director of Photography for the Minneapolis Tribune. He was instrumental in the development of the full-page picture story.

Mr. Harrington then spent twenty-two years as a staff photographer with Look magazine, doing in-depth color photographic surveys of entire countries, including Russia, China, and Africa. He was the first American journalist to enter Red China, in 1956-57, for which coverage he received the James Polk and the Overseas Press Club awards.

Following the demise of Look, Mr. Harrington engaged in free-lance commercial and editorial photography in the New York City area. He is still active in these pursuits, and in the meantime acted as the Graphics Editor for the Cincinnati Enquirer in 1974, was Associate Professor in the School of Art, Ohio University, and Chairman of the Department of Photography during 1972-74, was an Instructor of Photojournalism at Northern Kentucky State College in 1975, and taught at Union College in Schenectady, New York, in the fall of 1977.

For the past fifteen years, Mr. Harrington has been a specialist in the field of microphotography—the art of recording the world of the normally invisible on photographic film. His highly magnified "landscapes," "jungles," "abstractions," and industrial products are superb for their color, composition, and clarity. He has received numerous awards for his work, which include several from the Art Directors Club of New York.

Mr. Harrington has exhibited in many places—the University of Wisconsin, Ohio University, Nikon House Gallery, the Metropolitan Museum in New York.

He is a Fellow of the Royal Microscopical Society of England and a member and past vice president of the New York Microscopical Society. He presently lives with his wife and children in Brooklyn, New York.

Do you consider photography an art?

With that one question you've brought up a subject that we could spend days talking about. To give you an illustration: Two firms in North and South Carolina sponsor yearly art shows. One is the R.J. Reynolds Co. in North Carolina, and the other is the Springs Mills Co. in South Carolina. They have had a hell of a time making up their minds, "What is art?" Last year the Reynolds Co. included wood carving and things of that sort. The wood carving that I saw in the show was magnificent. But then I suppose someone on their board of directors asked, "Is wood carving really an art?" I think it is an art. But you get people debating it. The Springs Mills people said, "It's got to be painting or drawing, and nothing else." And in each case, they gave no thought at all to photography. In the case of Spring Mills, their conscience caught up with them and they have recently been funding some photography shows. But very seldom, anywhere, do you see paintings and drawings and photography hung together.

I was teaching for two years at Ohio University and was chairman of the Department of Photography there, in the School of Art. I had never given much thought to art photography. I'd taken it for granted. I discovered that the people at the University felt art photography was different from any other form of photography. They would not acknowledge that *all* photography, if it is done well, creatively, perhaps brilliantly, can be art photography.

I think it is true in almost any craft. It can be art if it excels.

I sincerely believe that those really fine photographers, who are considered art photographers, never thought of themselves as such. They wanted to do their thing, and they wanted to excel in it. They never started out to do "artistic" photographs. The current conception of art photography is philosophies and theories and mechanics that can be taught, and it has little to do with human emotion. I think all *true* art evolves from the heart and the soul. You cannot teach art photography. Particularly in formulas.

To give another illustration: When I was teaching at Ohio University, I found that any number of students were imitating Jerry Uelsmann. They worshiped Jerry Uelsmann. The instructor was encouraging them to do Jerry Uelsmann-type photographs. Well, if I've seen one tree root floating through the air, I've seen them all. Jerry does them very well, but his imitators don't. Then we had a clique of Les Krims photographers. I'm certainly not a fancier of Mr. Krims's style of photography, but he provided a niche in the photographic field with his approach. But God, it's an approach that should never be imitated. And then there was the third person who was imitated, Diane Arbus. We had all kinds of little Diane Arbuses running around, and they couldn't wait until the circus came to town so they could photograph the freaks. The instructors were saying, "Those are great. Those are wonderful. They're from your soul." Well,they weren't from anyone's soul. They were a ripoff of Diane Arbus's soul.

So art photography, as such, cannot be taught. We do our thing, and if we do it exceedingly well, the art world may acknowledge us. I take a dim view of art photography. I have pointed out to my classes, and I point out to you, that perhaps 90 to 95 percent of the deceased photographers who are accepted as great photographic artists made their living selling and taking pictures commercially, with absolutely no thought of turning out art photography. History and the passage of time has dictated that it's great photography, and important in photographic art.

The work that I am doing through the microscope, I feel, could in some ways be interpreted as photographic art, and I would like to think that someday I'll have a show or two of these pictures. But I'm not aiming for that. I'm going to keep doing my pictures through the microscope, commercially. As I explore the unseen world, I'll find elements that entice me to come back for more, and I'll work with that, and that will become my own expression.

One of the terrible things, Jerry, in the field of photography now is that almost no schools are teaching photographers to make a living. All of the schools that I know of, with the exception of the Rochester Institute of Technology and the Brooks Institute in California, are teaching photography as an art form. Many of those kids love photography and want to make a living at it. They tuck their art portfolios under their arms when they get out of school, they come to the Big City, and they're laughed out of office after office because they have nothing but imitation Diane Arbuses and Jerry Uelsmanns. They are not even communicating with their photography.

The first week that I was working at Ohio University, two people who had graduated the year before came in to see me. They had taken their portfolios to Chicago, and the portfolios were terrible. They were hurt. They were nice people. They heard that I was involved in applied photography, so they came back to the school to see if I could help them. All I could say was, "Enroll and take another two-year course. Take a graduate course, and I'll help you build up your portfolio so you can make a living." Well, they couldn't do that, but they had tears in their eyes. They said, "Why did we have to go through this? Why didn't somebody help us?" Well, nobody helped them because there is such a mystique placed on the words "art photography." I have no idea how this mystique started, but it has grown—to the exclusion of a great deal of good photography.

When I took the job as chairman of the department at Ohio University, the schism between those students studying applied photography and those studying art photography was a deep valley. After the first year, I learned that many of my students in applied photography were doing exceptionally well, not necessarily because of what I was teaching them, but because they were studying photography as an art form and taking a lot of that knowledge, putting it in the bag along with the material that I was giving them in applied photography, and shaking the bag up, and what was coming out was some pretty exciting commercial photography. That schism should not exist among the various fields of photography. There is fine photography coming out of almost every field of photographic endeavor.

One of the curators at the Metropolitan Museum told my wife recently that he felt the exhibit pictures of twenty-five years from now are the advertising pictures of today, because they reflect a whole way of life. There is where you have it. There are a lot of frustrated young people who have not been encouraged to communicate. They have been encouraged to contemplate their photographic navel. But they have not been encouraged to communicate.

Why do we become involved in photography? Perhaps because we are inarticulate, but we are sensitive souls and we have a need to communicate. So we pick up the camera, and we want to express our emotions on the photographic paper. Many photographers do it well. But we should never, never, never be encouraged to copy. A colleague of mine, a writer, is doing a magazine article on photography and photographers, and one of the questions she is asking is how many books on photography photographers have in their libraries. I have perhaps half a dozen. I have never been a collector of books on the subject, because I didn't want to be influenced by other photographers' work. I wanted to be cognizant of it. I'll go into a bookstore and brouse. But I don't want to be influenced. She said that she had contacted many professional photographers, and they all said the same thing. They did not have gigantic libraries. Many of them had no books at all on the subject of photographers' work. They didn't want to be influenced.

Let's talk a bit about photojournalism.

For years I was a photojournalist, working on a number of newspapers. Then I went to *Look* magazine and spent twenty years as a staff photographer.

I was looking at your article on Russia, and I have seen Burt Glinn's *Holiday* issue on Russia. They are distinctly different. I think that the photojournalist, or any photographer, brings himself to every picture he takes. As a consequence, each one is different.

If what you are saying is true, and I'm sure it is, you are assuming that the photographer taking those pictures is a sensitive soul, an extremely observing person who can record his observations.

Do you believe that successful photojournalists, who make their living as photojournalists, can be successful without that type of sensitivity?

Oh, yes. It's done all the time now. After I left Ohio University, I took a job as picture editor of the Cincinnati *Enquirer* because I felt that, perhaps, the future of photojournalism, as I knew it, was in the newspapers. When *Look* and *Life* died, we all knew that phase of photojournalism had disappeared; at this point I'm not sure it's ever going to be recaptured. So I became involved in newspaper photography again, as a picture editor. I had a staff which included about ten photographers. All of them were union members. Very independent. So it was very difficult, if I wanted to improve the quality of anything, to make any headway. They were protected by the American Newspaper Guild, and nothing but outright murder could sever them from the newspaper.

A number of photographers were graduates of journalism schools where they had studied photography. I was appalled at what, apparently, they'd been taught. They'd been taught that as news photographers—and they considered themselves photojournalists, but they weren't—they'd been taught that they could not use lights, that they should not interject their own feelings into the photograph. They should merely make a recording of an event with natural light. I found that difficult to understand. And the results were appalling. They were dull beyond belief.

I did a survey of three newspapers before I went to work for the Cincinnati *Enquirer*. I broke the news photography into categories—spot news, features, fashion, sports, and so on. I found out that spot news photographs accounted for no more than 2 to 3 percent of all the photographs that were published. Sports photographs took up perhaps 15 percent. The largest percentage of the photographs were devoted to women's activities and features. A feature photograph would be a photograph in which the photographer had little to work with. Perhaps an interview, where he had to photograph an individual. It could be a Ladies' Aid Society meeting, where there would be a group of older ladies in a room, and they were planning a bake sale. The women's department [of the newspaper] had said, "Yes, we will give you some publicity." In all honesty, the results of the bake sale would be more interesting than the women planning it. But there comes the challenge. That's why I put this picture in the feature category. What can the photographer do with five old ladies sitting in a room? He has to use his imagination, and perhaps he should use lights to make the picture more dramatic. Perhaps he should be more than just a snapshot observer of the scene. Perhaps he should become a director and direct the scene. After all, he was hired to do exciting photographs and images for the paper. I would point out that in all of those papers, the writers were given a great deal of leeway. They didn't record conversations verbatim. They often colored the story with their own opinions and observations. And that is considered legitimate journalism. I feel a photojournalist can also do this, particularly in a newspaper.

If he wants to photograph the five lovely old ladies for a story about their bake sale, he should consider this a challenge. What can he do? He has the five ladies and a bare room. So let's bring up the lights. Let's use some backlighting to accent their silver hair. Perhaps let's do a formal portrait of them to show their age. Let's make the picture more dramatic. Then, when it's published, it will have more readership impact.

Now why use lights? One reason, as I said, is to make the picture more dramatic. Another reason is to give the photographer more depth of field so the picture will be sharp. Thirdly, to take the murkiness out of the photograph so that it will reproduce better. So many photographs taken with natural light turn into murky, ink-smudged photographs in the paper. If the images can be made sharper, the more successful the photograph, the better it communicates.

If news photography is a continuation of photojournalism, a great deal of the person should enter into his news photography. But it doesn't. I'm talking about compassion, humor, and the thousand other elements that make up living, and make life exciting and interesting. But I pick up the average newspaper and I see, by and large, blurred images—more often than not, in a small paper, of people staring at the camera. So news photography was, to me, a great disappointment.

The fine photographs that have been done by the great photojournalists of our time have been obtained because they were willing to spend hundreds of hours with their subjects to the point that, as photographers, they would disappear into the wallpaper. They would become part of that person's life. That person would forget the photographer and be himself, or herself. Then the photographer could get pictures that were absolutely devastating, clinically brilliant. Emotionally strong and exciting. But he got those only because he spent a great deal of time with his subject material.

A news photographer cannot get a fine photojournalistic picture in a few minutes. He can get a news snapshot, but he cannot get something great. The fact that news photographers are unwilling to use accepted photographic techniques to enhance their pictures is a great mistake. But it's those techniques that are being taught in the schools of journalism today, including Ohio University and the University of Missouri.

How did your interest in photomicrography begin?

When I was in high school I wanted a microscope. My father borrowed our doctor's microscope. I went out and got some pond water. I didn't know how to manipulate the microscope, but I saw some wiggly images, and it was awfully exciting. So I carried that excitement with me for years. Finally, fifteen or eighteen years ago, I went out and bought myself a microscope. I worked with the microscope for a week or two and discovered that I was going to have to devote a great deal of time, effort, and money to find out how to use the instrument. In retrospect, it took an unbelievable amount of all three. More than I ever expected. So I could become the master of the equipment, and it didn't master me.

I found images in nature that I never imagined, in a million years, existed. I explored, and it was just as exciting as exploring the jungles of the Amazon. I could create my own little jungles. I could go down to the local ponds and bring back the seaweed and look at the little objects. Then, of course, I realized I knew nothing about the things I was looking at and that meant getting books about biology, diatoms, minerology, and on and on.

Things seen through the microscope have very little color. The scientist, more often than not, will stain his material. I had to learn how to do stains and smears, and so on. Then I discovered that I could use polarized filters and inject color into a great deal of my subject material, particularly things like rock sections and cross sections of wood. It would give me magnificent imagery. I discovered there were wave plates that are used in conjunction with polarizing filters to inject pastel tints and colors you couldn't get otherwise.

I became involved in the microscope just as a means to create and photograph visual excitement and visual patterns. But it's come to much more than that. I would say that a goodly portion of my income is derived from photographing imagery through the microscope. The reason that I get so much of that type of work is that the large corporations do not necessarily have scientists who are visually oriented. They are interested in looking for specific things under the microscope, not in creating exciting imagery.

The corporations or ad agencies come to me because they want pictures of the client's product, and they want them visually exciting. More often than not, they want them extremely colorful. I have devised many techniques to introduce color into the imagery, techniques that the average scientist knows nothing about because he is merely using the microscope as a means to scientific end. To me, the microscope is the end unto itself. I'm having a great deal of fun with the microscope, making a living with it and creating with it.

If I may just diverge back to photojournalism today. We have talked of the history of photojournalism and newspaper photography. The new picture magazines of today, such as *Us* and *People* magazine— the best thing you can say about them, although they are superficial, is that they do use photography. The sad thing is that they do not give the photographers any time at all to do a story. Their assignments average a day in length.

They do not have the budgets that the old picture magazines had, so the temptation is to use young photographers because they will work cheaply. The problem that we older photojournalists have is that the picture editors today, I think, feel they are insulting us by offering us work at $150 a day. The truth of the matter is that we do make more money working for corporations and industries, but we still love photojournalism. Although we are encouraged to use our photojournalism techniques in industry, we still like to use it as a true photojournalist on a magazine. They feel that we won't work for that kind of money. Well, some of us won't, but some of use will because we want to get back into that type pictorial approach.

What it ultimately comes down to is that you cannot do a story on a human being in a day. It takes three days or four days, preferably a week or two, to get to know that person and to record him honestly.

What about some of the new, specialized magazines like *Mariah* or *Quest* or *Geo*?

The problem with those specialized magazines is that they don't pay much. They would rather pay a young photographer a hundred dollars for a day's work than an experienced photographer three hundred dollars for a day's work. It's great to be young and be a photojournalist. It's hell to be older and have a family and children to support. You cannot support a family in today's economy on what magazines pay.

I see a diminishing in quality in magazine photography because the fine photographers are becoming involved in industrial and commercial work, and they are living well. But you don't see their work, or if you see it, you don't know that you've seen it, while the magazines are really propagating mediocrity, photographically.

What do you think of limited edition print selling?

The limited edition approach is, to me, such a harmful thing to photography. What it means is that if you are a reasonably good photographer and have a private income and can afford a good public relations rep, he can make you famous and he can sell your limited edition. Not based on quality, but based on the worth of your name. The greatest living photographer in the world may be completely unknown to us at this time. No one is going to handle him because he doesn't have a name.

This is incidentally, Jerry, a problem which we former magazine photographers have. We were names at one time and we are no longer. We had the glamour of the expense account, the glamour of the world-wide trips, and for many of us it's been awfully difficult to make the adjustment to the world of reality and scrambling. Some of us scramble well and some don't scramble well at all.

Which do you consider more effective, photography school or apprenticeship training?

I think school can be much better than an apprenticeship. Not that I'm demeaning apprenticeship, but I think it means learning the techniques of only one person. One of the traps you fall into as an apprentice is learning the techniques and not the esthetics of photography. I think there should be a generous blend of both. An ideal situation is one in which you learn the esthetics of imagery and the mechanics of putting the image together. I believe that one of the reasons my students were doing so well in the second year at Ohio University was because they had been immersed in the esthetics and they came to me and learned a lot of the mechanical techniques that gave them the freedom to express themselves esthetically. The lights and lenses and everything else should be tools in our hands to get that final effect we visualize.

I don't see any evidence that any of the schools are teaching anybody how to go out and make a living—the business involved, the problems of selling yourself, meeting the clients, hiring a rep, or finding a rep.

None of that's being done anywhere.

How would you improve the method of teaching?

I wish there were photography work-study programs, in which a photographer could study for a month and work for a month. I think that would be the ideal situation. There's no reason why programs like that can't be formulated.

Photographers, for some reason, do not communicate much with each other. Art directors and graphic artists have all kinds of clubs and they hold conventions and meet together and talk about their craft. Photography is such a secret thing. Photographers are afraid that if they get together with each other, they will spill trade secrets. My friends won't even tell me who they're working for, for fear that I will steal their clients away from them. A few of us have agreed to exchange clients' names with each other, because if someone else gets the assignment, I would rather it be a friend of mine than a stranger.

Do you do your own processing or do you have it done for you?

I have it done. Some of my prints are dye transfers, others are type C prints. I'm just becoming interested in having some of my prints done on Cibachrome paper.

In your microphotographic slides and prints, are the colors we are looking at the colors you see through the microscope, or is there some manipulation in the printing process?

No, there is no manipulation in the printing process. For years I worked diligently trying to get as complete color saturation as I could. I found that by using 120 Ektachrome X color film I could get the type of saturation I wanted in my pictures through the microscope. Now I'm looking for ways to make my coloring more subtle. My clients are starting to say, "We want natural color." Right now I'm involved in an assignment photographing thin sections of fossilized coal. The client said, "There's too much color. It doesn't look enough like coal." So instead of taking a microphotograph through the microscope, I am going to take a macrophotograph of the thin section and use colored gels to make it an intensified brown. The sections are actually beige in tint.

The problems I have in microscopy are several. One is getting a flat field. In scientific photography through the microscope it's desirable to have the field flat, from edge to edge. Flat-field objectives are extremely expensive. Cheaper objectives have what is referred to as curvature of field. The center may be sharp as a tack, but the peripheral areas will be soft. So what you end up doing is using just the center area. That may change your magnification. Whereas you used to be able to buy a good microscope objective for a hundred dollars, now the price for a good objective is anywhere from $1000 to $1500. I can't pay those prices. I recently ran into a client who objected that the picture wasn't *quite* as sharp as he had expected. Yet I know that to get that little bit of additional sharpness will cost me at least $1500.

This brings up the problem for the average photographer who might want to take pictures through the microscope. He will have a difficult time getting equipment. Used equipment is hard to find. New equipment is prohibitively expensive. For a person wanting to start out in photomicroscopy, I would say he needs an absolute minimum of $500, preferably a thousand, to get the equipment. Even with a thousand, he or she is not going to bring much equipment together. The camera equipment that sits on top of the microscope will run from three hundred to a thousand dollars per unit. Five hundred dollars will buy you a tolerably good used microscope these days. Then, when you are thinking in terms of sharpness, you're thinking in terms of thousands of dollars. It's dangerous to go into a hock shop and just buy a piece of equipment. A young person had better settle himself with an experienced microscopist who will assist him or her in purchasing equipment.

My recommendation is that a person should contact the New York Microscopical Society, headquartered at the Museum of Natural History, and ask them for advice. There are still a few persons who sell used equipment that can be trusted. The problem with the used equipment market is that basically there isn't any. You seldom see microscopes showing up as used pieces anymore.

How do you do your color staining in the microscope?

Years ago there was a system invented by old Dr. Rheinberg in Germany, a system of optically staining material. Since then it has been known as the

Rheinberg system of optical staining. It consisted of doing nothing more than putting little colored circles underneath the stage. There is a center-spot and a peripheral ring. Used in juxtaposition, you can make the background go one color, and the subject material go another color. I have built some of my own filters, and I can make the subject material go three colors.

This optical staining method can be done very cheaply. These circles are nothing more than cheap gels cut out. But then the Germans came out with a very sophisticated system of optical staining. It is called a Mikropoly-chromar. It consists of the microscope condenser and a lot of paraphernalia. This gadget, which is probably seventy years old, has become a collector's item. It's not available any more.

There is also a polarizing technique. I have a polarizer and an analyzer in this Leitz Ortholux microscope, and I'm using wave plates. By inserting these wave plates, I get different color combinations. Now this gadget was made perhaps seventy-five years ago, and no one makes anything like it anymore. So I just insert this antique gadget into the light path of the modern scope and I get the effects I want.

I have Nikon scopes, the Leitz scope, and the Olympus. I much prefer the Olympus scope to any of the other scopes I am using. Of course the Leitz scopes are lovely, but they have become prohibitively expensive. The Olympus scopes can still be afforded, and their optics are superb.

Is most of your work transmission, or do you use reflected light also?

I use a lot of reflected light. I usually use fiber optics, and I'm having some condensers built on the tips of my fiber optics. I have various systems of lighting.

What is your basic light source?

I use, basically, tungsten light sources. The newer scopes have quartz halogen lamps in them. Now the quartz halogen lamp gives you a balanced Kelvin output at any intensity, which you don't get with tungsten lights. As you diminish the intensity of a regular tungsten bulb, the light becomes warmer and warmer. That's not true of the quartz halogen lamp. You can diminish its intensity and it still retains its 3200° or 3400° Kelvin rating, which is a blessing.

But I don't worry about Kelvin ratings. The fact is that in doing a great many of my polarized light photographs, I find that I can use either day-light film or tungsten film and get exactly the same results. I discovered it by accident. I'll use daylight film and forget to use a conversion filter, and do half a roll, and discover that I forgot it. I'll put it in and finish shooting, and discover that the results are identical. When it comes to polarized light and light through optical gels, the light source and the film don't seem to make much difference.

How do you determine your exposures?

I have here an exposure unit which is sold by *Science and Mechanics* magazine, and no matter whether it tells me a 30-second exposure or a

1/125 of a second exposure, the exposures will always be right on. It is extremely sensitive. At full power, it can read the light going through my thumb. Of course it has to be calibrated initially. You don't have f stops on your microscope, so the only variables are the intensity of the light and the shutter speed.

Here is an example of why this business is so expensive. I have a cheap 35mm camera hooked up to what is referred to as a focusing telescope. The focusing telescope mechanism, which fits over the microscope, will run anywhere from two hundred to a thousand dollars.

One of the problems that we have working with the microscope is that some subject material is so "contrasty" that the film cannot accommodate it. Other subject material may be extremely flat, in which case I'll want a contrasty film. I often use so-called photomicrographic film from Kodak. It also has much finer resolution. Resolution-wise, it's finer than any other color film on the market.

It's known as Kodak 2483 and is rated ASA 16.

Right. Incidentally, the new Ektachrome films are giving us a great deal of trouble. The new Professional Ektachrome has to be refrigerated until time of exposure, and then afterwards, too. Most of us find that the amateur Ektachrome films are much superior, much more stable color-wise. The new Ektachrome films have not given me the results through the microscope that I have had in the past with the old E-3 process films.

How do you find the images you are now making to be different from your early microscope work?

My early work through the microscope is a reflection of my excitement with my subject material. There was very little thought given to the esthetics of what I was doing. Many of my earlier works I find glaringly bad. I am now getting into things which are much more subtle. I'm doing more of this type of thing, and I think I can tuck some of my present work under my arm and take it up to the Museum of Modern Art, believing in it, and saying I believe in it and I want them to buy it. Or I could take this up to one of the galleries and say, "This is the kind of work that I'm doing, and can I have a show?" A much more simple imagery has evolved out of the complex imagery that is so visually exciting under the microscope.

Lance Jeffrey

Fashion photography has probably received more publicity in recent years than any other photographic field. Avedon, Scavullo, and Newton are as well-known as the designers whose work they photograph. What does it take to break into the ranks of the famous? What kind of person has the courage and push to enter a field as competitive as it is glamorous?

The career of Lance Jeffrey provides one answer. Not only is he succeeding, but he is doing it from a late start. He is a self-taught photographer; his natural abilities have been cultivated and nourished by his tremendous drive and confidence.

This award-winning photographer works out of his large loft studio in Manhattan.

How did you get started in photography?

I started when I was a kid, as a hobby. I guess I really started to get into it when I was in college. As a college student I did a lot of traveling. I always had a camera around to document what I was doing and with whom. I got fed up paying people to do my processing and I started doing my own black and white. It developed into, I would say, an advanced hobby, with a darkroom in my apartment. I picked up a few little jobs here and there from friends and relatives. I didn't think of it seriously as a career. It was just a hobby. That's basically how I started.

When did you decide that photography was *the* thing for you?

I figure it was 1972, roughly, that I started taking pictures of the Kennedy family for Ethel Kennedy at the pro-celebrity R. F. K. tournament at Forest

Hills. I gave up being a schoolteacher, which I was from '69 to '75. I gave it up in '75 and got myself this studio. Actually, it was a raw loft, close to 4,000 square feet. Prior to that I had decided that I was going to give photography a fling. I wasn't making any money as a schoolteacher and was definitely not enjoying it. There is no gratification, no satisfaction, no appreciation, *nothing* in teaching. So I got the loft. It took me three weeks to put this place together. It was sort of incredible.

You worked your butt off, didn't you?

I worked my butt off, twenty hours a day, twenty-two hours a day. I did everything systematically. If I did the ceiling, I could do the walls without waiting for the ceiling to dry. Everything went like clockwork. I had plumbing put in, I had all the electricity done, and I put up all the walls, put in the kitchen, did all the floors, the studio, did all the preparation before I moved in. It was done and quite livable within three weeks. for all intents and purposes, I am still adding. I am forever putting in another door, another wall, or better lighting, but for all intents and purposes the studio was finished quite a while ago.

I then spent about six or eight months testing, learning about lighting, studio lighting, testing with models, getting to know the modeling agencies. When I felt I had enough of a command with enough equipment, I began to take my portfolio around, myself.

In your opinion, can photography be taught?

I taught photography, but I taught mostly darkroom. You can't teach somebody how to take a picture. They are going to shoot what they want to shoot. You can teach them the basic skills for using a camera. They are going to frame what they want to frame. They are going to overexpose or underexpose to their liking. You can teach what the *f* stops mean, the times of exposure, all the workings and workmanship of a fine camera. Then you can teach darkroom procedures, how to improve upon your picture in the darkroom. If you flub it more or less out in the open, how you can fix it up in the darkroom. Or how you can do different things, how you can take parts of a picture and print it up, and so on. That you can teach somebody. You cannot teach somebody what to shoot, what they are going to like. Each person has his own mind. It's like a professor saying to you, "This is a course, and I want you to repeat it to me verbatim." There is no individuality. You can teach the basics, but that's about it.

I gather then that most of your knowledge of photography has been self-taught?

It's *all* been self-taught.

When you were doing your own work, when you first developed your portfolio, how did you determine what you ended up with? In other words, were you influenced by the responses to your style as you took your portfolio around? Did you modify according to the remarks?

This requires a full answer. There are two ways of starting photography as a fashion photographer. One way is probably the proper way. You begin as an assistant, working for experienced photographers. You work for them for a year or two—you learn lighting, you learn how to deal with clients, you learn studio procedure, you learn what's the best functional studio, you learn what's the best functional darkroom. You learn what equipment is best, what holds up under certain conditions. Then you learn also what you should have in your portfolio. That's the proper way.

Then there was my way. I was too old to start working for somebody as an assistant. I already had obligations and expenses that I had incurred as a poor teacher. I had to make money immediately. I began everything by myself and learned the hard way. I took my own portfolio around. I did my own testing, I learned my own lighting and my own studio procedures. I built my own darkroom. There are a few things that have had to be changed over the years because it wasn't as functional as I thought when I originally built it.

So there are really two ways of going about it. One is working as an assistant and one is doing what I did. I would not advise the average person to go at it as I did. I mean I have more drive and more persistence than the average person, so I would suggest that if you want to learn something about photography, be an assistant to someone. Friends of mine have told me that it has taken them five to eight years to accomplish what I have done in two and one-half or three years.

What type of equipment do you work with?

I use 35mm and 2¼. The 35mm is all Nikon, *all* Nikon. I stress that for two reasons. One, they have been most reliable to me in six or eight years of hobbying, knocking around, dropping, and studio work and fashion photography. They are reliable, they don't break down, and they have an incredible system—I can use all different kinds of lenses under any circumstances. Point two, which is not as important, but nevertheless is important: A client paying a lot of money for a day's shooting wants to see Nikons. He's paying for that privilege. For 2¼ images I use Hasselblad equipment, and that's the best.

How did you end up in fashion photography rather than some other discipline?

I started to accumulate lenses and lens boards and bodies for a 4 x 5. I was going to do still life photography. I was doing it, and experimenting in the studio with a friend of mine who is a still life photographer. I felt that bottles were a little boring, and that product shots were getting a little dull, so I decided to do a little testing. The easiest thing to do was to test girls as opposed to bottles and stuff.

I had a portfolio put together of some still life, some scenery, and some fashion. I figured I'd take the book around and see what got the best response. I started getting work from department stores and lingerie companies, which started to push me into fashion. I dropped the still life, sold the still life equipment, and picked up more 35mm and 2¼ equipment. I stuck with fashion and it has been very good to me.

Do you still shoot for your own pleasure?

Yes, quite a bit. I still do scenery shots, infrared shots, time exposures, skylines. When I go on a trip, I'm like any other tourist. I went skiing in France over Christmas and New Year's and I took thirty-odd rolls of pictures just of the Alps and the people in the town, the snow and the skiing, and my friends and European friends. I'm a tourist, like everybody else. I use the camera as a record to document my trip, hoping the company that supplied the film will buy some of that stuff, which they said they would.

You know, a lot of it is grab shots. You happen to be in the right place at the right time. Basically, I still do shoot a lot by myself. Whenever I go away for a weekend, I usually throw a camera over my shoulder. I have a camera that I can get sand and water on, so I have a camera that I can obviously take to the beach.

In fashion photography, what is the key factor that determines what you are going to do when you make a photograph?

95 percent of the time you work from layouts. You are always working with an idea from the art director. Usually they specify. If they leave it up to your creativity, you obviously want to get the garment in. The garment is what is being photographed. If you are working with a big model, it's important to have her face in it and make her part of the image. For example, if she is on contract with a makeup company, then obviously you want to get a shot of her. She is what is important with the makeup. It really depends on the art director and the model and the garment. There really is no set answer. You want to get the garment in. That is very important. But you might not be shooting for a garment. You may be shooting for a watch. She may have her hand across her face to display the watch or bracelet. You want to see the face, you want to see the blouse, but the watch is the most important. It can be any one of half a dozen things.

There was a short article recently in one of the photography magazines that said, basically, that fashion photography has gotten so much publicity during recent years that it has become very self-conscious. Its purpose has gotten lost in the adulation of the photographers. You have been in the field during this period. Do you think there is a tendency for fashion to become a vehicle for the photographer's ego, rather than the photographer being a tool to show fashion?

Yes, I would definitely say so. Some of the companies and ad agencies would prefer to hire a big-name photographer and pay him $3500 or $4500 for one shot and give him a by-line. For example, Avedon or Scavullo, or somebody, just to shoot one simple shot. I wouldn't say *any* other photographer could do it, but any good photographer could shoot it. They are not just selling the garment. They are selling the fact that Scavullo did the shot, or that Avedon did the shot.

In other words, the ad agencies or the clients themselves are selling the photographer as well as their own product.

Exactly.

Is there a lot of work around?

There is enough work floating around for everybody, if you can get it.

How much infighting is there in your particular field?

Well, actually, any kid with a camera is a potential hazard. You go to a small business and the president or vice president has a niece who has a son who is an amateur photographer. That amateur photographer might end up shooting a layout for a trade publication or something for which he would charge maybe $50. A professional could come in and do the job right the first time and charge $500 or $1500, but you get a professional job.

In all cases it is not true that you get what you pay for. A lot of the kids are going to keep shooting and shooting and shooting until they get something that the client can possibly use. In my case, if a client calls and asks me to do something, I'll shoot it and he will get what he wants the first time around—if the client knows what he wants. You do run into clients and art directors who don't know what they are looking for. Or they know and can't convey it to you.

Does a client ever come to you without any format or any layout? Do you ever do the layout work?

I don't necessarily do the layout work but I have, in some instances, given quite a few suggestions as to location or how it should be shot. I've done some work for a big department store in the city. I took all the merchandise and was more or less on my own in the Virgin Islands, to go ahead and shoot as I wished. For that I won a creativity award from *Art Direction* magazine, which is a sort of judging by my peers.

I would say that I do contribute a lot to the format or layout, if in no other way than with suggestions. I can suggest the models and locations. A lot of times the art director or the client leaves no opening. They want you to shoot this, with this kind of camera, and probably with this kind of lens and that kind of lighting. You have to follow that exactly. This is also a talent, to pick up something that somebody else wants done and be able to duplicate exactly his thoughts. He may not be able to express his thoughts, which is even a trickier thing. He will tell you but he is not really expressing what he wants.

Which way of working do you enjoy more?

Obviously, I enjoy being more creative. When it comes to creativity, I'd like to be a little more creative. But it doesn't always hold that way. You've got to do what the art director wants. He's the guy paying you.

If you were conducting this interview, are there any questions that you would ask Lance Jeffrey?

Well, I guess one of the things I would ask myself, "If I had to do it over again, would I do it as I have?" Yes, I would. Probably, if I had a choice, I would rather have gone to work for a photographer and been his assistant and learned the ropes that way. I thing it's a little more difficult doing it the way I did. But I've got a lot of push and a lot of drive, and I'm doing it.

Jay
Maisel

Jay Maisel lives in a six-story ex-bank building in New York City. Not on one floor. In the entire building. The first two floors are his gallery. Nobody else's. Just his. If you like color photographs you won't find any better place to see them.

Mr. Maisel was born in Brooklyn in 1931. He studied art with Leon Friend at Abraham Lincoln High School, and then painting with Joseph Hirsch in 1949 and at Cooper Union Art School in 1952. He holds a Bachelor of Fine Arts degree from Yale University, 1953. About that time he discovered he liked photographing more than painting. He took a photography course with Herbert Matter in 1954 and has been a free-lance photographer ever since.

He has sold to magazines, advertising agencies, and directly to major corporations. He has taught photography at the School of Visual Arts and at Cooper Union, both in New York City. He has lectured at the International Center of Photography and the Royal Photographic Society in London, and for the Professional Photographers of San Francisco.

Mr. Maisel's prints hang in numerous private and corporate collections. He has been in group exhibits in New York City at the Metropolitan Museum, the Museum of Modern Art, and the Museum of Natural History, as well as the Baltimore Museum, the Smithsonian Institute, "Man and Planets" in Montreal, the U.S.I.A. Exhibit in Rumania, and the Nikon Image, a traveling exhibit.

He has had one-man exhibits at Photographers' Gallery, New York City; Limelight, New York City; the U.S.I.A. Exhibit, Russia; Hemisfair, San Antonio; Focus Gallery, San Francisco; Cooper Union Alumni Gallery, New

York City; Nikon House, New York City; Silver Image Gallery, Washington; In and Out of Focus, a WNYC television show; and the Alternative Center for International Arts, New York City.

Portfolios of his work and articles about his work have appeared in Modern Photography; DU (Switzerland); Contact; Popular Photography, Camera (Switzerland); Life magazine's "Gallery"; Japanese Design Quarterly (Japan); Audience; and PHOTO (Italian, German, and French editions). His photos have also appeared in a number of books. All of the color photographs in Harry Golden's The Greatest Jewish City in the World (Doubleday) and Jerusalem (Time-Life), came from Mr. Maisel's cameras. Another book, San Francisco, is soon to be published by Time-Life.

Do you ever shoot anything besides color?

Yes. I used to shoot a lot of black and white. I don't anymore. I shoot some, privately. But not really for an assignment, except when they ask you to shoot black and white *and* color, which I usually fight, but if they'll pay extra for it, yes.

You don't like doing black and white?

No, I don't like doing both together.

Why not?

Because you've got to think one way or the other. When you are shooting a job, certain situations that would work in color don't mean anything in black and white. So you have to change the situation. Certain situations are reversed. They're going to be nice in black and white and in color they're going to be a bust.

Do you think of some subjects in black and white and others in color?

I think of almost everything now in terms of color. I'm not sure that is apropos. It's just personal for me.

Do you make most of your income on assignments now, or do you make a big chunk of it selling prints?

It's a very increasing curve of the prints. I've been laying money into it now for almost fifteen years without even any real effort to sell them. They were just things I wanted to print. I would use them to show people for commercial work, and have them for myself, privately. Now it's beginning to return. On a sharply increasing curve.

All your print work is dye transfer?

All the things that I sell.

Do you sell them as numbered editions?

Yes. Large limited editions. Not thousands, but hundreds. I try to standardize things. I don't want to do prints in nine different sizes. I do want to do things in two sizes. I think things make different kinds of statements in different sizes. The way I've started to work it out is that I've made a very large selection of a number of different prints. I've made them very small, and for a very reasonable price. Later, they will be made into very large prints, at very unreasonable prices. So that the people who got the first set at the reasonable prices won't feel hustled because somebody else got it later. I try to make it known that the first thing will be small and will be an edition of one hundred and it will only be $100, and then later, when they are made large, it will be an edition of 150, and I figure $1500.

When you say "large" . . .

I am talking 40 by 60 [inches].

Do you have any comments on how photography has changed over the twenty-odd years that you have been in it?

I think it has gotten better. There is such an influx of people. There's just an incredible explosion of numbers in the field. I think the general level of photography has gotten much better.

The business is another story. The business was much better years ago, in terms of what you were able to do. The editorial market has gone. It didn't affect me. I was never able to work for *Life*, for instance. I've done books for them, but at the time that *Life* was in its heyday, I never could get work from them. I almost never solicited anybody that I had a hard time with. I once spent a week in BBD&O's office, trying to get a job there, because it was the only major agency I hadn't worked for. It was a matter of ego. I tried, and it didn't work out. That's about the only occasion I can think of where I actually solicited somebody who didn't solicit me.

Basically, there is no forum anymore for any kind of picture essays or picture stories.

Did you do that kind of work?

Yes. I did some things for *Esquire* and others.

Looking at the work in your gallery, I got the impression that most of your work comes from your eye for the individual picture more than for the picture essay.

Well, I don't think they have to be mutually exclusive. Basically, I did very few picture stories because I couldn't get that kind of work. It was somehow easier for me to get brochures and ads, and when I wasn't doing brochures and ads, I worked on my own things. I've always worked on things that I want to work on, whether they were jobs or not.

What do you shoot with now?

I shoot with Kodachrome. I find that I have to test the film a lot now. I didn't have to do that years ago. Now I have to test every batch.

We've totally changed in the last twenty-four years from black and white to color. The reason I started in black and white was because, well, you shot black and white. Nobody did color. The reason I went to color was that it became more exciting for me, but the reason that I *kept* shooting color was that it became pretty obvious that everybody was shooting color. There was no longer any reason to shoot black and white unless you had a love affair with black and white, and I had a love affair with color.

I still like black and white. I think it's marvelous. But it means spending hours in the darkroom. It means giving up some things I like visually. So I stick with color.

Do you shoot everything in 35mm?

Everything. Well, 99 percent.

And you are getting 40 x 60 pictures out of that?

Yes. In fact, I have gotten eight-foot by twelve-foot black and whites out of 35mm.

It's not me. It's there. It's a hell of a lot better quality if you are doing it with 8 x 10s, but I don't think you have any question as to which is more flexible. If you can use 35, you have a great deal more flexibility.

How much personal shooting *do* you do?

A lot. I don't do projects. But I shoot personal whenever I can. If I am doing a job for somebody, I'll try to grab a day for myself. Or I'll be shooting all day for them, and at the end of the day I'll grab some film and shoot for myself. Or I'll shoot for myself around here.

It's nice to have an assignment to shoot something on, because it motivates you to do it more. But, I really . . . I sort of sneak it in, for myself.

Do you have all your printing done outside now?

Yes.

How much of your time is spent on photography, and how much is spent on running your business?

Interesting question. A lot of people are coming around for interviews, it seems like.

It's getting to a point where I can spend the whole day just doing administration things. I don't like to do it, because it eats into my time.

Most of my time is spent editing. You can shoot for an hour, and edit for a day. You can shoot for a week and edit for a month. I just did a job for United Airlines, a fourteen-day job. I edited about forty-two hours. I keep a log of my editing time. That's five eight-hour days, and that's just my time. That doesn't count the time of the people who work for me, who set the film up, take it out of the boxes, put it in other boxes, turn it right side up, label it, and then send it up to me.

How many transparencies do you shoot on a job like that?

I shot 260 rolls. That was easy to edit, because the film was so lousy that anything that was marginal got tossed right out. Sometimes you get stuff that is not quite what you want because the light wasn't just perfect, or the composition was slightly off, but the film quality is so great that it's worth giving it a second thought. Well, in this case it wasn't. . . . So it was very easy to edit.

How much freedom do you have in your shooting? Do you work to art directors' specs?

You have as much as you want. You don't have to take the job. I don't want excessive freedom, because then I'll never come back. I'll be out there shooting forever. I want to know what the parameters of the job are. I like a guy to give me *some* parameters. I like him to give me the subject matter and tell me, "I want the best you can do. I don't want anything less than the best you can do."

If he tells me I have to follow the layout, I usually tell him I'm not very good at following layouts. What happens is that I get hooked into following the layout, and I forget about the picture. It's not that I'm a prima donna. It's just that I know if I start to follow a layout, I'm not going to give the guy the best job I'm capable of. I don't do much planning. I know one guy who used to shoot the entire job with a dummy model. Process it, print it, and make a whole presentation, and ask "Is that what you want?" That is very valuable to a client, but I'm not that kind of a guy. I'll go out without any damned idea what I am going to do, because I want the thing that I am shooting to motivate me.

Sometimes somebody gives me an assignment, and I say, "Wait! That's *too* much freedom." Somebody wanted to send me to Africa, and they said, "Shoot whatever you want." I said, "Wait a minute. You're going to run me a double-page spread in a big magazine. I don't want to come back with fantastic stuff and hear you say you're not going to like it." He said, "No. Whatever you want." Now there is a kicker in every job. The major thing I wanted was real representation of each country I went to. The kicker in that one was, for instance, the Sudan. The Sudan is bigger than all of Western Europe. I had to nail it to some degree, to some kind of subject matter, or I would be running from dawn to dusk and not have any chance of doing any kind of real presentation. So we tried to limit it.

How do you sell your work? Do you use a rep?

I don't have a rep. There is nothing wrong with having a rep. If you want to make a lot of money, you should have a rep. But I never have been shy about dealing with business people. I think it's part of the fun, "hondeling" with people. I like to know who I am dealing with, what kind of people they are. I don't need to be shielded. I can talk with company presidents. It's not an irksome task. It's fun. These guys got there by being intelligent people. And it is interesting to talk with them.

I also like delivering my own work. I love showing my pictures. It's an ego trip, if it's good. If it's not good, you find out why it's not good and you don't have to get it from somebody else. You get it from the guy who decides.

How often are you satisfied with your work?

My wife doesn't understand that. I was reading something about the top insurance salesman in the country. There are clubs for guys who sell one million dollars a year, guys who sell five million dollars a year. This guy sells something like 62 million dollars in a year. That makes him at least thirteen times better than the other guys. And he says that one of man's greatest abilities is his inability to be satisfied with anything he has.

There are things I like in retrospect, and there are things that I'm very excited about when I do them, but I never feel that I've done exactly what I wanted to do. I think it is one of the "secrets" of success. The inability to be satisfied. And yet, I know people who are good, who are totally, totally delighted with everything they have done.

I'll give you a feeling that I have, in a nutshell. If you're taking terrific pictures all the time, you're not trying hard enough. It means you are taking the kind of pictures you've taken all along, and you're not trying to stretch yourself further than that and, consequently, you never fail. So if you never fail, it's tough to grow.

How did you make photography a success for yourself?

We were talking about that the other night. I just got a very big job. The biggest job I've ever gotten in my life. The biggest in terms of scope and money and the possibilities of doing a fantastic job. I'm very excited about it, but if the truth would be known, I'm not half as excited as I was when I sold two pictures to Fawcett Publications at $16 each, in black and white. That was my first sale. Then I sold a picture for the cover of *Dance* magazine. Then I got an assignment to do a two-week dance festival for *Dance* magazine. Then the art director of the magazine, whom I had become friendly with, gave me the names of a few people in New York. I went to see a lot of them, and Neal Fugida at Columbia Records gave me a bunch of album covers. And things kept coming along, and it grows. . . .It's like a snowball.

How much homework do you do for an assignment?

I don't do a lot of homework. I don't believe you should. I was reading an interview with Ernst Haas and Harold Sund, about how they shot the "Cities" jobs. Harold did Tokyo and Ernst did Venice, and I did Jerusalem and San Francisco. They were talking about how they prepared, to get an overall concept. Harold walked around without a camera for five days. Now Harold is terrific. I think he's dynamite. And Ernst is one of my heroes. But I don't work that way. I feel that if you walk around without a camera for five days, by the time you get the camera in your hands, you've lost five days. You've lost five days of excitement that you are never going to have again 'cause it's that much more familiar to you. I want to walk down the street and get hit with things I never dreamed of. I want to walk down all the wrong streets and find things I wasn't supposed to find. Eventually I'll get the layout of the city. I'll understand what it's about. And I'll shoot it.

If you were interviewing Jay Maisel, what questions would you ask him?

Interesting. I've done that. I've started writing these things called "Interviews with Myself." I'd probably ask me questions I couldn't answer.

What questions can't you answer?

"What would be the ideal assignment?" "What do you want to do when you grow up?"

What has been your most exciting assignment?

I think the one I told you about in Africa. I went to a lot of countries, had a lot of trouble. . . . Seeing things I had never seen before. Getting back to the homework thing, I don't like to prepare myself too much. I like to have an idea, am I heading west or east, but I don't particularly want to know which block.

I did something on Baja, California. That was a very nice assignment, and that was laid out for me, like, turn left at the third cactus and go ahead . . . and it was still terrific. It was just very exciting, because they couldn't possibly tell me what was really going to happen. They didn't even know themselves.

Let's get back to that other one. What would I ask? "To what would you attribute your success?" Hard work. The reason I say this is because it's within the grasp of everybody. I don't want to tell you that there is some little secret that, if I tell it to you, everything will be within your grasp. There is no little secret. I will bet money that I put in a harder day than anybody. I may come down in a bathrobe at ten, but I was up until six o'clock in the morning working.

I think that a certain amount of talent is also a prerequisite. I think your ability to see the picture that others don't see is important.

I don't know. The toughest thing is to have perspective. I look at my work, and I know all the failures. You see the successes on the walls, but I know all the failures. I assume that anybody who puts in the same amount of time to produce the same amount of failures will have the same amount of successes.

That's debatable.

I think the difference between the amateur and the real pro is that . . . they come along and shoot something and they're finished. I come along and shoot it . . . and I go back . . . and I go back again. . . .

You can see it defined. I was standing by the edge of the Grand Canyon. A guy gets out of his car, he walks up next to me. He looks down. He takes a shot and he puts the camera back. He goes in his car, and he drives away. I'd been there for four days, and I hadn't gotten a shot! I got some nice shots, but to this day I don't think I've gotten anything that's really great of the Canyon.

I went back to Times Square every New Year's Eve for seventeen years. I got better stuff the first few years than I ever got later. I don't know what went wrong. I just never felt I got a really great shot. You just have to go back again and again and again, and you have to keep doing it.

Again, it's tough to have perspective on yourself. The shots that I remember most clearly are the ones where the camera wasn't ready, or the wrong lens was in, or I was driving too fast and I didn't stop, and then I did stop and I went back and it wasn't there. The shots I got, I take for granted. The ones I miss are the ones I never forget.

How much luck is involved, do you think? How much is luck and how much is your ability to see the right moment?

Luck could be defined as persistence. I know one guy who got a shot like that, and everybody said, "Wonderful shot, Jack, terrific shot. Boy, you were lucky!" And he said, "You know, the harder I practice, the luckier I get."

Are there any assignments you wouldn't take?

I would not do feminine deodorants. I think that's the worst thing in the world. I wouldn't do anything that I thought was politically immoral. I would work for any party, from any part of the political spectrum, but not if I disagreed with their morality.

Fred
Mullane

Fred Mullane is a young, successful photographer who has specialized in the field of sports photography. More photographs are probably taken by more photographers every day in this field than in any other, with the exception of snapshot photography. Most sports photography is repetitive and basically dull. With a subject matter that flourishes because of the excitement involved, it seems as though its photography should be equally exciting. Mr. Mullane manages to achieve this excitement with a combination of superb technique and often brilliant timing. His photographs are recognizable for their unique impact, which explains a great deal of his growing success.

His biography is better presented in his own words.

How about some basic biography?

I'll be 30 in two days. From Newark, New Jersey. Mostly lived in New Jersey. Went to St. Vincent College in western Pennsylvania. Studied English literature.

Nobody studies photography, huh?

I've known only one guy who's been successful, and that's Pete Turner. See, the problem is that, unfortunately, the current trend, with perhaps the exception of two schools, is to teach these people to become photographers—artistic photographers. Or they teach them, as Rochester Institute does, highly technical background, but they don't teach them anything about business, they don't teach them *anything* at all about how to deal with clients, how to relate to people. So either way you are on the short end of the stick.

What was your own training?

Magazines, and just doing it. What happened was that, like so many people, I had a million hobbies, coin collecting, etc. But I got a camera the summer of my sophomore year, took it down to the shore, photographed all these *lovely* girls. I went back to school, and I was paying some guy a buck to develop the film. He said he would teach me. I thought, "This is great." He taught me, which took all of two days, and I started shooting for the yearbook, which was marvelous, because if you shoot for a college yearbook, you get all this free film and paper, so you really get not a great background technically, but it helps you eliminate a lot of steps, because you are not spending your own money to learn, you're spending the school's money.

I was studying English literature, knew I couldn't teach, didn't ever want to teach, so I thought, "Perhaps I'll be a writer." That seemed relatively easy. At that time. I've since learned otherwise. But, naturally, since I didn't have enough training, I figured I would take the classic approach and go to work for a camera store, which so many people do who want to be photographers, because you get discounts on the gear and all this, and maybe you get free film, or at least half off. And that held me up for a few years, but at the same time I learned a good bit. I learned how to deal with people, in selling cameras. I also ran a mail order, so I learned very quickly how to relate to a lot of different types of people, which in many respects is much more valuable than any photographic training that you are going to get.

You have to deal with clients, you have to deal with subjects. When you work as a salesman for your livelihood, if you do it for a few years—I did it for four years—you learn how to sell yourself. Which is, I would say, at least 85 if not 90 percent of what photography, as a business, is all about. 10 percent is photography. That's all. Unless you are really into studio stuff or really bizarre stuff that is so specialized that nobody else can do it, you're selling your personality, because there are a thousand guys, a million guys out there who can do the same thing. So they want somebody who gives them the least grief, who's fun to work with, and who still gets it done.

Do you have a studio of your own?

No. Most of the time I'm on the road. I would say 90 percent of my work is sports.

What's the other 10 percent?

Oh, photojournalism. House magazines, easy type of stuff. Now, within the sports you have editorial and you also have advertising. But you are still shooting the same event, or the same type thing, just for varying degrees of money. The other would be simple things, such as going to Bowie Kuhn's house and photographing, or belly dancers in front of the New York skyline. Standard *Us* and *People* photos.

What kind of sports work do you do?

I shoot tennis, skiing, baseball, horseracing. I've shot badminton, table tennis, racket ball, squash, fox hunting, which is one of my favorites. I shoot for *World Tennis*, for CBS Sports on "60 Minutes," *Us* magazine, *Raquets Canada*, *Ski Canada*, *German Tennis* magazine, *Japanese Tennis* magazine, Head Tennis Company, Bancroft, New York *Times*, *Sports Illustrated*.

How do you sell yourself? Do you use a rep?

I do it myself. I've been looking for a rep, and have more or less decided that if I get one, I'm not going to get one in New York, I'm going to get one in Chicago, and hopefully Los Angeles. Because I can cover New York now. Most of my work is now coming out of here, so what I want to do is get somebody out in the Midwest and in California. Because there are a lot of fertile markets that you don't touch if you stick strictly to New York City.

How did you end up doing most of your work in sports? Was this your own interest or did it just happen that way?

Well, it's my interest, but what happened was that I was still selling cameras and I was down in Washington. A friend of mine was teaching me to play tennis. Teaching me in the sense that he would hit me with the ball every day at lunchtime until I learned to do reflex volleys, and this sort of thing. He was playing in tournaments, and I said, "Well, I'll go shoot some photos of you." And I went to this tournament and shot it and thought, "Well, this seems pretty easy." They were having an indoor tennis tournament down there, and I conned the tournament director into giving me credentials, under the guise that we were testing lenses, for one day. I kept the credentials for a week, took the photos, and sat on them for about three weeks, didn't think they were all that good, and finally decided, what the hell, might as well take a shot. I sent them to *World Tennis* magazine— its offices were in Houston at that time—and got back a great letter from the editor saying, "We would have considered them for a major layout. Next time, send them right away." So when they had another tournament in Washington, I called the editor and asked, "Can you give me credentials?" He said, "No, but we'll give you a letter." I got the letter, went, got the credentials, shot the tournament—and about two months later hit the cover of a magazine. I think, "Well, hell, this is going to be real easy." Hah, hah. So I decided, more or less then and there, that I would shoot tennis, and move on from there to other sports. I thought, "Well, this is great. I can cruise in and in six months I'll be on a staff."

It doesn't work that way, of course. But it just sort of blossomed from there. It has taken a while. I guess it takes about two years, in New York City, before people will even talk to you. They won't hire you, but they won't even *talk* to you until you've been around for two years. Just, I think, because they want to see if you have staying power. If you can make it through two years, then they figure, well, the guy's not a complete bum. And then at least they are willing to look at your work. It might take another year, then, for them to hire you. It's a long process, like anything else. I think you need to go through your dishwashing period. I think that's very important.

I know you work basically with Canon equipment. What specialized equipment do you use?

Just long lenses. I just read an article in a photo mag where a guy was saying that to shoot tennis, you use from an 85mm to maybe a 135mm. Most of my tennis work is 200, 300, 400, 500, 600, 800mm. With the 135mm I might make $60 to $70 a year. Sports, in general, tend to be very long-lens stuff. We shot a particular player the other day for *Sports Illustrated*. The shortest lens I used was a 200. I would say the bulk of the stuff I shot was with a 600. And, if it was daylight, and I could have gotten 800 or 1200, I would have used that. That would have been better. The tighter you are, usually, the more impact your photo has, within reason. If you get *too* tight, you tend to abstract a little bit too much.

I also use motor drives quite often. Sometimes, in indoor tennis, with the men, you can't use a motor because they are just so finicky. But the bulk of the time, you use a motor.

What films do you work with?

Outdoors, Kodachrome, unless I really have to use Ektachrome. I hate to do it. It really makes me sick. As a comparison, it's terrible. There is no contest whatsoever. Tri-X or Ilford HP-5, most of the time. Sometimes, a slow black and white, but most of the magazines just don't like it because it gets a little too blocky. For the work I'm doing, most of the time, it's pretty high-contrast stuff, and it just blocks up a little too much. It doesn't print well. It might print all right as a fashion piece, where you have the time and get the spread. But for tennis, or for football or baseball, it's just too hot.

Most of the equipment you describe is for outdoor sports only.

I shoot a lot of indoor stuff. Football, the Super Bowl, are indoors. Tennis, a lot of indoor tennis.

So with the long lenses . . .

300, 2.8s; 200, 2.8s.

Indoors, you have to work with Ektachrome.

I work with Ektachrome, and you're shooting it at 650 or 800. Sometimes more. But once you get past 800 with Ektachrome, it's shooting craps. You might get it and you might not. So if you can shoot it at 800 and stop the action, great. 650's better, but. . . . Unfortunately, most of the places are lit like bathrooms, so you have to catch as catch can. There, usually, the 300mm, f 2.8 is as far as you can go, unless you have a real hot lens, and there you're talking $3000, $4000.

Do you have to work with team managers or team publicity people? When you are shooting football, for instance.

All right. In football, what happens most of the time is that the magazine gives you a credential, assuming that it's a magazine you are working for.

Unless you are doing a specific thing, normally you wouldn't even be involved with the P.R. people. You wouldn't get involved with the manager at all. It would be with the public relations office, if anything. Again, it might depend on the publication you are working for. Some publications carry so much weight that, even if you don't want to, you're going to meet the guy. And a lot of times you don't want to, because they can influence a situation a bit too much. Sometimes, in a lot of cases, I guess, the players really don't care for these guys. . . . I've seen that on numerous occasions—they want the athletes to do things that they just don't want to do, but the athletes have no option. I've seen it even in amateur sports. So if you can stay away from those guys, most of the time, you try.

On the other hand, though, sometimes they can be a great help. If you are going to work with a particular athlete, and you need to get his cooperation, then you have to go through these guys, set up a time, etc. It's like greeting any dignitary, you know, you have to get your audience with the Pope, and you get your twenty minutes, or whatever it is that you are going to get, and in that time, try and get the guy to do what you want, or a semblance of what you want. In those cases, usually, the art director or the photo editors design the shot. You have to come back with that particular photograph. Unless it's a game photo. But a lot of times, it's something that you have to set up, have to stage. You need the guy's cooperation, and you have to work through the P.R. people.

When you are shooting game photos, how do you set up a shot? Are there particular things that you look for, anticipating that this is going to give you what you want?

Yes, a lot times. In tennis, for example, if you are going to do a poster. I had to do a poster last year of Villas, and the company that I shot it for didn't want any clothing logos. And if you think about that, it makes it very, very difficult because it eliminates almost all of the shots save one, because the guy's body has to be turned around in such a way—he's got one logo on his shirt and one on his shorts—so even if the top of his body is turned, a lot of the times you've got the leg logo. You've got to get the right shot. So then you have to really watch the guy for a little bit and think about it. You've got to design the photograph before you take it. Even though the guy is running all over the place, there are certain elements or patterns that are predictable in any sport, whether it be football, baseball, basketball. You are going to get a certain repetition. So you have to really study the sport. Even if it's the first time, you've got to spend ten or fifteen minutes watching the guy, seeing how he turns, whether it's a man or a woman, seeing what's going to allow you to take that photo.

Say you are going to shoot Chris Evert, and you want a backhand. You don't want her head down. She tends to close her eyes on the shot, and you don't want that. So you have to hit her where it is going to be a high backhand. She's going to have her body turned around but her head will be looking up. You really have to watch, and you have to shoot it just at the precise instant when you have all the elements—if you want to have the butt plate of the racket showing so you can see the company's logo, that sort of thing. It's a question of timing and of understanding sports. You don't have to know all sports. You don't have to read through books and that sort of thing for hours and hours and hours, because once you shoot two or three sports, I think you understand enough about competition and athletics that it won't take you very long to come back at least with something usable, which is the name of the game. You might not be the best at it. But you'll come back with something every time. That's what the magazines pay for, consistency.

Do you do all your work on assignment, or do you still go out and shoot on speculation?

I would say 90 percent assignment, 10 percent spec. You have to spec a bit. There is no way around it in sports. If for no other reason than to build up your stock files. And to get used to doing different sports that you might not see that often. Or just to become familiar with something. Like soccer. I want to go shoot soccer. I'm going to try and go shoot a Cosmos game on Sunday. I've never seen a soccer game, except on television. And I'm told it's very hard to shoot. But, of course, I'm told everything's hard to shoot; so we'll see. Usually the people who tell you that are the guys who are the only ones shooting it, and don't want anybody else to do it. You know, they told me tennis is *really* hard, and skiing is *really* hard, so you better not shoot it. As it turns out, skiing is a lot easier than tennis.

Have you ever shot polo?

No. But I doubt that it would be too difficult. I've shot horses, and I understand how polo works. Probably the easiest thing would be to line up behind the goal with a long lens. At some point the guys are going to have to come charging into you. And you've got it. It might take you twenty minutes or a half hour, but you'll get it. You'll at least get *that* shot and, if nothing else, that's the classic polo shot. So you're all right. You're covered. All sports have a goal. Whether it be golf or whatever, there's a certain sense of direction, there's a certain sense of movement. If it's a skier, it's downhill along a certain line. If it's tennis, the ball is going to be put on a straight line to something. If it's golf, you're always driving, you're always shooting forward, toward something. So you keep that in mind. Football, the same way. Basketball, the same way. You are always coming toward something. They have to score a point, and there is a way to score a point. That is to reach over or into a certain boundary. As long as you are aware of that, and figure out some way to position yourself so you are going to get that forward movement, or at least some movement coming toward you, you are going to come back with it. *All* sports.

A good point. What was your most difficult assignment?

I would have to say the Super Bowl. Not in terms of photographing, but in terms of the kind of pressure you have to work under. I shot for a network, I was the only one there covering for the network, and I had to do party photos. Twenty-six rolls of party photos. You know, the sort of cocktail party with so-and-so, the president of this, and so-and-so with this advertiser, and then the game. And when there is only one person to cover the game for a network, or even for a big publication, the work is very, very difficult. 'Cause you've got to get everything. I like to work under that kind of pressure, and I think you'll find that most guys who work for a living, especially in New York, really like that kind of pressure, that kind of edge. You need that competitive edge. It's a lot like sports. You'll go out and practice. You have to keep your timing. And you also have to have that constant edge, that pressure. It's like magic. It's almost like being on the field, the same thing. If you go to the Super Bowl, sure, you've got a group of guys out there beating their brains out for a lot of money. You also have 100 to 150 photographers who are doing the same thing on the sidelines— exactly the same thing. It may not be that you are coming up with a greater shot, but it's your going for the money. It's the Super Bowl of sports photographers too. You have to be there. It's a hot credential. In sports photography you have to have the hot credentials, in the sense that if you're seen at enough of these really big events, it lends a hell of a lot more credibility to what you are doing, and that will get you jobs. It's very simple.

When you shoot the Super Bowl, how much homework do you do?

None. What is there to do? What homework do you have to do? I know the sport, I know what happens. God knows, I've been punched in the face enough. I know what happens when you play the game. The only thing you can do beforehand as far as homework is to call the arena and find out what kind of lights they have. That is a big consideration. Once you get that done, you can't do that much homework, 'cause you have to go there and find out what the light's like, and usually it stinks. You already know what film you're using, but you don't know how bright it is going to be. Superdome tends to be a cellar. So that's a problem. The sport itself is the least of your problems. The football game is fairly long. Even though it's a one-man deal, you're going to use enough cameras, at least three, so that even if one breaks down, you're going to have photos from the other ones, so you are going to have shots.

So you just have to struggle. You just have to run around. You have to climb the steps. You have to get up on top of the place. You have to get on the field. You have to run up in the stands. You have to shoot the crowds. You have to cover the whole game. But that's part of the job. That's what you're being paid for. So it's no big deal. It's just the pressure of having to get it all. Plus having to shoot the parties, which can be wearing, far more wearing than the football game.

Shooting the parties. How do you schedule those? It seems to me that would involve a lot of homework. You have to know who you have to shoot.

What you usually do is shoot with one camera, maybe two. You get your automatic flash with a battery pack, usually, 'cause you're going to shoot a lot of photos. You wear your suit and stuff your pockets full of film, without looking too much like a buffoon. You have to look neat. All right, I'll give the whole rundown of the weekend. Fly down on Thursday. Friday you have a meeting about eleven o'clock with the woman you work for. At about two o'clock they have a reception. You go and shoot that. She's with you and you photograph people she points out, plus the people you recognize. Obviously, there are sports commentators you know, so if the guy is with somebody, you shoot him with the person. You pretty much have to shoot everybody. That breaks up about five. You go back to the hotel, maybe take a shower, change your shirt. Change into a different suit, if you're that rich. You leave, go back to the hotel, shoot from seven o'clock to one. In this case, they had two game rooms and a major party room. You have to cover all that, running into one room that's in another building, not part of the hotel. After the first night, you pretty much know who the important people are. What you do is, you have to get them. You have to kind of glad-hand them, you have to get those people to be shot with everybody. People say, "Naw, I don't want to be photographed." Really, they do. You just have to get them to smile, and then bail out fast. You take your photo, that's the key to that, you take the photos, you take two shots, never just one, because a guy may close his eyes, or make a face, so you take at least two photos, and get out of there. If you stay any longer, you're not going to be able to shoot them again, or you're going to put other people uptight. You've got to keep moving. Got to keep smiling. All the time. Smile, smile, smile. That's the key to the thing, and that's part of the job also.

Next day, Saturday, same thing. Early in the morning we had a football game with the commentators. So you go and you shoot that. Then you go back and change. Then you have another party that goes from two to five. Shoot that. Go back to the hotel, change. Then you have another one from seven to twelve, and you shoot that. Bail out. The next morning you get up and shoot a breakfast from ten to two-thirty. Go back to the hotel. Change into your working gear. Go right to the stadium. The game starts at five, you should be there no later than three o'clock. This is true of all sports. You should get there early, well early. Check things out. If the guys are practicing, maybe you can get some photos. A lot of times you can get the photos you want while they are practicing. They're a little looser, or whatever. Plus you can work closer.

You go to the game. Shoot the game from five until whenever the hell it ends. Then you have a party directly after that, so you don't even go change into your suit, you go upstairs and shoot the party. You shoot this until, say, ten, and then you bail out, go back to your hotel, and with any luck maybe you'll have something to eat. I didn't have my first meal until that breakfast before the game, and that was after we had finished shooting. The next morning at eight, catch a plane out.

That's quite a weekend.

Yeah, but that's what they are all like. Not so many party photos, but if you go to an event, if you go to World Cup skiing, you have to get on the slopes at seven in the morning, shoot them running the course, or you get your position. The photographers who can ski, ski the course, or walk the course, and see where they can shoot. In skiing, you want to get blue skies, so you need a gate just below the crest of the hill. Maybe ten feet below the crest of the hill, so you get the blue skies, no background, and the skier, also the feeling of moving downhill. If you get too much farther down, you have all white, and it tends to flatten out, and you can't see that it's on a mountain. It's a bad photo. You need to have that sky. That's where the homework is. You just have to get there early and take a look.

How much risk is involved in this kind of work?

You mean getting hit by a football player? That's not risk. Covering war is risk. If they send you to Vietnam, or to Cambodia, that's risk. Getting run over by an athlete, that's not risk. Granted, you can fall down when you're skiing, or when you're up on a mountain. But I don't see that much risk. I'm not talking about mountain climbing or anything like that, because that's a hazardous business on its own.

If you were conducting the interview, what questions would you ask yourself that haven't been asked?

I guess the classic is, "Would I do it again?" And if so, "Would I do it the same way?" I would do it again, but I would change things. I would have gone into it a lot earlier, realizing now the length of time it takes to establish yourself. I don't think that you need to be an assistant to anybody. You can teach somebody to use a camera, but you really can't teach them a feel for certain things. If somebody shoots sports or fashion or photojournalism, they have a certain feeling for moments in time, and that's what photography's all about. It's the isolation of time. That's why still photography will never die. It does something that nothing else does, including painting, and that is, it takes an instant, a *real* instant, and just extracts it from the air. You can create the instant or you can find it. A lot of times, by putting yourself in the proper place, I think you have created it. You're not simply finding it. That you can't teach somebody. It's what makes a good photographer or a bad photographer. It becomes a matter of timing and reflex. Six people with motor drives could still not get the right instant. You have to anticipate that precisely. That is something you can't teach.

Earlier you said you wanted to comment on Pulitzer Prizes.

Pulitzer Prizes! My God. Why is it that photographers who work for magazines and who do annual reports are not given the credit? Why is it that unless you work for a newspaper or a wire service, you cannot get a Pulitzer? Your work isn't as good? Look at some of the guys that shoot for *Time* and *Newsweek*. You mean to tell me that these guys aren't as good as, say, Brian Lanker from Topeka, or Michael O'Brian from Miami? Now I'm not saying that these guys are no good. I have tremendous respect for their work. I am saying that I think it's time that, just because a guy works in color, or works for a weekly, you shouldn't say his work is not as valid. I think a lot of people have been done gross injustices. Larry Burrows, one of the all-time great war photographers, dies in Indochina. He never got a . . . thing. And he's recognized by his peers as being one of the great war photographers, but he didn't work for a newspaper, he worked for *Life* magazine. So what does that make him? Just another hack who shoots Ektachrome? It's not right, and I think it's unfortunate.

Do you do any shooting strictly for your own pleasure?

That's one I'm having a lot of trouble coming to grips with. I used to. I used to do it a lot. I've just started trying again. I've got this mental block now. Unless I'm being paid for it, I just don't shoot it, or I don't see it. I'll walk down the street and I'll see things, but they won't move me enough to do anything. Yet, you give me $200 or $500, and you'll be *amazed* at the things I'll see. I find a certain block, and I guess it's something you go through. You go through certain dry spells. You don't go through so many with your work, you go through dry personal spells, either from lack of motivation, or you're putting so much of yourself into your work, and the tension that devolves there, that you almost have to withdraw a little bit. You have to put the stuff down and not go shoot. But you need to do personal work.

I'm not an artist. I don't purport to be an artist. There's a big difference between being an artist and being a professional. You *can* be both. But if you are going to be a professional, you can't strictly be an artist, and I'll never purport to be one. I want to be a professional, I am a professional, and that is my prime interest right now.

Who does your processing?

Kodachrome, of course, is done by Kodak. Ektachrome, it depends on who the magazine has an account with.

Do you do any of your own?

Oddly enough, I'll develop the odd roll of black and white myself. It's like getting the Kodachromes back. Once I see the negatives, I see what's on them, I know I've got it. So then I give it to somebody who can do it a lot better than I can. When I see that strip, I know it's there. Then for me, the job is done. I can wash my hands of it. I'm a photographer, not a printer. A lot of people disagree with this. They say you should do your own black and whites because it's part of the process. But do they take their Kodachromes into Kodak and say, "Hey, I'm here to run the machine now. . . . It's the shot that counts. Once you get it, you don't have to stick your fingers in the Dektol to finish it. There are half a dozen printers in New York City who can blow everybody else in the world away, with the exception of Ansel Adams. Hell, let them go for it.

Ruth
Orkin

During my interview with her, Ruth Orkin never made the statement, "If you want to do something, do it." I don't think she would. She would be too busy "doing it." As a successful free-lance photographer in a time when the idea of a woman being a photographer, and particularly a photojournalist, was just not considered, she simply did it. Actually, of course, it wasn't simple. Her energy and enthusiasm have not been diminished. Her eye for the world around her, as evidenced by her stills and movies, is warm and positive, in the best humanist tradition.

Ms. Orkin is the daughter of silent film actress Mary Ruby, and was raised in Los Angeles, where the potentiality of the movies as a form of expression became a cornerstone of her artistic personality. After a bicycle and hitch-hiking trip across the country in 1939 at the age of seventeen—"Because I wanted to see the World's Fair and that's the only way I could afford it"—Ms. Orkin, in 1943, became the first female messenger at the studios of Metro-Goldwyn-Mayer. By then she was a confirmed photographer. Since her intention of becoming a cinematographer was met with laughter—the idea of a girl getting into the union—she decided to become a still photographer, because there was no union governing that field. In 1944 she came to New York to become a photojournalist. The problems she overcame are discussed in the interview.

She met and married Morris Engel. Together they conceived and produced two children, Andy and Mary, and two movies, The Little Fugitive, which took the top award at the Venice Film Festival in 1953 and was nominated for an Oscar, and Lovers and Lollipops.

Ms. Orkin's photographs have appeared in Life, Look, This Week, Collier's, Ladies' Home Journal, Coronet, Esquire, Cosmopolitan, Horizon, New York, Ms., and many other magazines. They have appeared in ads, trade books, textbooks, and photo annuals.

She has had one-woman shows in New York City at the Witkin Gallery and Nikon House, and at Enjay Gallery in Boston. She has been in numerous group exhibitions at the Museum of Modern Art and the Metropolitan Museum of Art, in New York City, including "Family of Man," "Color," and "Young Photographers."

Ms. Orkin is represented in the permanent collections of the Metropolitan Museum of Art, the Museum of Modern Art, the Museum of Fine Arts in Houston, and the New Orleans Museum at Art.

She has been featured in several magazine portfolios and photobiographies. She appeared on television on the "Today Show" in June 1977; "In and Out of Focus," 1974; and on CBS Television in 1950 on the Museum of Modern Art show.

She lectures and teaches. She is represented in New York by the Witkin Gallery for prints; by the K&L Gallery for large mural-sized color prints; and by G. Ray Hawkins in Los Angeles.

At the present time Ms. Orkin is working on a series of books, built from her photos and her life. The first, published in the fall of 1978 by Harper and Row, is called A World from My Window. It features fifty-five color photographs and twenty-five black and white, all taken from the window of her Central Park West apartment.

In the works are One Little Boy and How He Grew and One Little Girl and How She Grew, photographic and written diaries of her children. In addition, A Collection of My Best Photographs, A Collection of Magazine Picture-Stories, What I Saw ... And Did, Bicycling Through America in 1938-39, Classical Musicians at Rehearsals, The People of Israel, The Little Lifeguard, and The Little Fugitive.

How long have you lived in this apartment?

Twenty-three years. I came to New York during the war, in 1943, and I lived in two other apartments first. I lived on Horatio Street in the Village, and on West 88th.

When you rented this apartment, was it in anticipation of the photographic possibilities?

No, I just wanted a view, a view of the park, so that it would be like Los Angeles.

How many pictures have you shot from this window, would you guess?

In twenty-three years, I would say thousands.

You do very little shooting anymore?

If I can possibly help it, yes. It's that this is [motioning toward the window] so enticing. You know, it's hard to resist.

You were instrumental in getting magazines to use 35mm color.

Yes. The first 35mm slide ever printed on a slick magazine cover was one I took on my own. It was on *Ladies' Home Journal*, March 1950. No one would touch anything smaller than 2¼ in those days. You can't *know* how many magazines I kept showing 35mm color to before that got printed. It was only because John Morris at the *Journal* pushed and made the publishers and printers do it. It doesn't seem like anything today, but it was a milestone then.

Do you do any of your own processing?

Not any more. I had ten years of it.

Yet, when you teach, you insist that everybody do his own darkroom work.

Well, it's like learning the piano. You have to keep your fingers positioned a certain way at the beginning. Then, later on, you can do what you want to do. I had somebody in the first class who had the nerve to send his pictures to the drugstore, and they were *color*. I can't teach photography that way. After that, I put in the School of Visual Arts catalog, along with "No Smoking," "No color and must do own darkroom work."

Is your longest lens still 135mm?

Yes. When a friend loaned me a 500mm I was able to get just the top of the Sherry Netherland Hotel from here. It's in the book. I also filled a slide with the roof of the Plaza Hotel looking like gold. Pure gold, because of the way the sun was hitting it. It was just gorgeous.

Why don't you get a longer lens?

Then I'd be at the window *all* the time!

Why don't you pick up one of the new, small zoom lenses?

Because I don't want to keep my old Nikons. I want a new, small compact camera, and I want some manufacturer to give it to me. I need to spend my money on *other* things.

You don't take a lot of grab shots just for sorting later?

Not usually. But it depends upon the situation. If I feel it isn't going to change, I take my time. If I know it's going to be fleeting, naturally I don't. When you see a group like that [looking out the window, pointing to the street below], it looks interesting at first, but nothing is happening, there is no focal point. I tell myself, don't shoot, because it just won't look like anything when I see the slide later.

Back in '59 you were voted one of the Ten Best Women Photographers [by a nationwide poll of photography editors and writers]. How did you feel about that at the time?

The fact that it was *women* didn't mean anything to me in those days because it was before the women's movement. I didn't think much about our being discriminated against. I accepted it. I grew up brainwashed, although a little more rebellious and adventurous than most girls in the thirties and forties. And another thing. I was really uninterested, because by that time I had made two feature films and I wasn't shooting still pictures anymore anyway. I was bored by stills.

Are you still bored? You can't really be bored by still pictures if you shoot all those thousands of pictures out of your window.

Yes, but this isn't photojournalism. This is just shooting out of my window. Anybody can do that.

I don't believe that.

It just took a lot of patience. It doesn't take skill, it doesn't take a lot of experience. It doesn't even take fancy equipment. Thirty of the fifty-six color pictures in the book were shot with a 50mm lens, and twenty with the 135mm. What it takes is patience and an eye. You don't have to be a photojournalist to do it. To be a photojournalist takes experience, skill, endurance, energy, salesmanship, organization, wheedling, climbing, gatecrashing, etc.—*plus* an eye and patience.

I gather that all your life you've been shooting and then going out and selling your work. Do you ever do anything on assignment?

I'd say about 50 percent was always on assignment.

This was after you became successful?

Yes. In fact that is very little, for a lot of photographers. Most magazine photographers made almost all of their money from assignments. The only reason, it seems to me, that I didn't was because I was so interested in shooting certain subjects that I would rather spend my time doing that than running after assignments.

That really is the question I was asking. A lot of your shooting is for your own pleasure, even though you hope to turn it into a living?

Well, only sometimes. Nowadays, selling is mostly an afterthought. Even years ago the "Girl in Italy" shot was part of a sequence she and I did mostly to amuse ourselves. Although, at the same time, I have these mixed feelings. On the one hand I'm often shooting for me, and on the other hand I feel it's a waste of time to take pictures if they're not published where a lot of people can see them, because my main purpose in photography is to communicate, to say, "Look at this" or "Look at that."

I went to California last summer for six weeks. If it hadn't been for the fact that Kodak came out with this really fast color film, ASA 400 Kodacolor, I would have just shot with the Instamatic. In the past, whenever I went sightseeing, especially with the children—in Washington, D.C., Philadelphia, Seattle, Montreal, etc.—I never took my Nikon for tourist shots. First, it's too heavy, and then if I have a good flexible camera in my hands, I feel compelled to get a really good picture. That's just too time-consuming. So last summer I took the Canonet and I just had a ball. I was shooting through the car window at 1/500th of a second. I shot all the old places I'm homesick for and all the new places that are fresh and interesting to me. I happen also to love all the things that sophisticated New Yorkers make fun of, like shopping centers, freeways, swimming pools, palm trees, giant supermarkets, and crazy architecture.

I put the pictures in a scrapbook and I showed it to *Westways* magazine and they're going to run four pages. Originally, the pictures weren't shot with any thought of selling them at all. They were shot for me (although I shot a few more for the magazine at the editor's request).

Do you see things differently when you are seeing them for yourself, as opposed to when you are seeing them for somebody else? Is your eye still the same?

Yes and no. But the subjects, you see, were for me. Places like the ladies' rooms at I. Magnin, and the Beverly Hills Hotel. Then I shot a cheap cafeteria, the Broadway, that no one in Hollywood or Beverly Hills would think of eating at. It's on Broadway in the old district of downtown L.A. But I remember, when I was a little girl, a string quartet from the Los Angeles Philharmonic that played there every day at 5 o'clock. There are colorful Spanish murals and beautiful tiles and ironwork that are still well taken care of. The quartet doesn't play anymore, but I still love the California cole slaw.

Do you think you will end up in Los Angeles, since you like it so well?

I'd like to. The trouble is that all the book publishers are here. I went out this April because I had a show at the Hawkins Gallery.

[At this point, I looked through Ms. Orkin's California scrapbook.] What these pictures prove is that the camera is not very important. It's the picture you frame.

I showed this book to my cousin in California, and she said, "I don't see why they want to run these pictures. They just look like any snapshots that I would take." Not everybody sees what you see! But I think she responded that way because I was shooting straight pictures of everything she's familiar with. She doesn't say that about my New York pictures. I once won an international color contest, by Kodak, because, I think, I was very careful to only submit pictures that looked as if amateurs could have taken them.

This is a spectacular shot. Look at that sky and the colors on the buildings.

People don't realize they have views themselves, you know? Look at the way the shadows from those buildings fall. It must be great if you stood there and really did it right.

I think *you* see the light in the right place. I'll bet that nine times out of ten if the light isn't right you don't even see the view. Don't you think so?

That is true . . . very true.

One of the most beautiful views, or times, or feelings, I ever got out of a window, I never shot pictures of, even though I had the camera. Because the lighting probably wasn't right, or the composition wasn't right. It was in California when I was sixteen.

In these shots, there are fewer people and there is more . . .

Composition?

Composition, space, place . . .

That's 'cause it's color.

You look at scenery and architecture *that* way and you look at people in black and white, I mean as far as shooting is concerned?

Well, it depends upon the situation. Yes. The minute you have to shoot people in color, you have to *really* pay attention to what colors they have on. Otherwise, the most beautiful shot of expressions and composition can be ruined by the colors being in the wrong places. So you are much more limited when you shoot in color, and especially—well, this goes for black and white too—I rarely shoot a picture in the sun, with people, but here you can shoot in the sun. You can shoot architecture in the sun. You need it, in fact.

Do you do your own selling, or do you work with a rep? Does Witkin Gallery handle much of your work?

Witkin handles any prints. Books, I do. I do have a book agent, but she is not interested in handling everything. The subjects are all so different from one another.

Do you have a photo rep?

I never have had, no. I always felt that being a photographer was 90 percent being a salesperson. Then, and today.

Being a photojournalist meant that you never had to have your own studio.

That's true, but then you also get paid less for ads. You know, the bigger front you can put up, the bigger the price. Or the bigger money you can get into.

Some of the first pictures you did in New York were done in a night club in Queens Plaza, to support yourself. How long have you been supporting yourself with your photography?

Mainly, I would say from 1945 to 1955. After that most of my income came from the two films, and from stock pictures. All these books [in-

dicating a set of scrapbooks, all large but of about equal size] have clip-
pings. There is 1945-49, 1950-51, then '51-'52, '52-'53, then see what happens
in '54? I made the movies in '52 and '54, so what happens then? It takes
more than six years to fill one book. And here it's another seven years, and
here it is two years, but that's because of the shows. Not many new photographs. It's just shows, lectures, exhibitions, interviews, and reviews.

**What this means is that you built a hell of a good base back in the early fif-
ties.**

I guess so. Well. Look at this. These are all musicians and they are the
most outstanding soloists and conductors of their day. I have candid picture sequences on each one, in rehearsal. And I feel that they are great
historical records for people who are interested in classical music. And I
hope they'll be in a book some day.

Are you still interested in doing movies?

I can't think about it now. At the time I made them I had a lot of ideas
and I thought I was going to make movies for the rest of my life, but then
unforeseen circumstances came into play. Mainly it was because I think
women's lib didn't come along soon enough for me.

**You have said that a couple of times and yet, without it, you certainly have
done things you wanted to do more than most women, at the time.**

You mean like being the first messenger girl at MGM? Well, they did it
only through necessity, because all the boys were getting drafted. They
never thought of hiring girls before.

**You are quoted as saying "Being a housewife and a scenic photographer at
the same time was an ideal combination." Obviously, you were a photographer long before you were a housewife. How did you adapt to the
change?**

It was a *shock*. In fact, before I had the baby I was afraid that I would
forget it was in the house and just leave it alone some day. But then I discovered that anything like that was impossible. You just don't forget that
there's a baby in the house.

And since then you don't forget it and now you enjoy it?

Well, watching the kids develop was fascinating. But enjoy being a
housewife? How can anybody enjoy doing housework?

I don't know. You spoke of it as being an ideal combination.

That's only because you've got to be around a lot to study scenery in different light. And here I was, home all the time *anyway*. That's all I meant.

Do you miss doing the photojournalistic work you used to do back in the days when, as you said, there really was photojournalism?

I did for a while, but not anymore. I think making movies is much more exciting and has more potential for communication and for reaching people. I regret the fact that I wasn't able to continue.

You rode your bicycle across the country. Why?

Because I wasn't rich enough to do it any other way! I was seventeen and I wanted to travel. I wanted to see the 1939 World's Fair, and we were on relief. The Depression wasn't really over. But I didn't bicycle the whole way! The newspapers just made it sound that way. I did 2000 miles in four months, mostly sight-seeing in the biggest cities after New York, and all through New England where the first youth hostels were in those days.

Richard Halliburton was one of my heroes. He wrote travel books and then came home every once in a while to give lectures about his adventures. David Douglas Duncan, in his first book—his spirit, his curiosity, his interest in everything—reminded me very much of Halliburton. He wrote letters back to his mother all the time, like Halliburton. I did too, and my mother saved them, but I later threw them away. (I didn't see her for five years, from twenty-one, when I left home, until I was twenty-six.) I decided that I was never going to write my autobiography anyway; I was just a photographer. Now I'm sorry, because one of the other books I'm doing is sort of an autobiography of those early Hollywood and New York years with all the memorabilia I *didn't* throw away. I realize now that I was a terribly busy kid as a teenager, and into a lot that would interest other kids today.

You spoke of "photojournalism when it *was* photojournalism." What happened to it?

Well, I feel that it's a tremendous loss not to have the big picture magazines, because it was a means of communication that you almost don't have any decent substitute for. The circulation was so big. You knew that if something got published, a large percentage of the population got the message. Also, it gave your work prestige. And it was really reaching so many people. The same thing doesn't happen on television because it's so quick that you forget. You can't hang onto it and hold it in your hands. Half the time you're listening with half an ear.

I think there's room for both. I think if they could get over the economic problems of getting the big picture magazines back, they would have millions of faithful readers, just as they had before. The picture magazines serve one purpose. Television serves another purpose. They should never cancel one another out.

Back in the era of *Colliers*, *Saturday Evening Post*, *Life*, you didn't have thousands of little specialized magazines.

They don't fill the bill. They don't fill the hole at all. They're just an addition.

Don't you think, even though they don't serve the same purpose, that they have taken a lot of the market that used to be there?

I don't care about that. I feel about it the way I felt about Mitch Miller. When they took Mitch Miller off the air because he had fewer viewers—only 30 million!!—than the next station with some awful western, I got mad. I feel that millions of people wanted *Life* and *Look* just as they wanted Mitch Miller. I used to enjoy hearing all those songs and I resented losing them.

You set up a lot of your sequences?

There are certain things you can handle by setting up the pictures, and for me they are totally legitimate, because they would have happened anyway.

You mean like this picture over here of the girl walking through the streets of Italy?

Yes. She and I were trying to do funny pictures for ourselves, just to show what a hard job it was to be a tourist alone in Italy, when all the posters were making it seem so glamorous.

What have been some of the major downs in your life as a photographer?

Not being able to buy a good camera. Having to borrow cameras. I didn't have a decent camera until I was twenty-four. When I was ten, I had a 39-cent Univex. When I was fourteen, I had a dollar Brownie. At sixteen, I finally got a $16 reflex camera, but it didn't have an anastigmatic lens. That was all I had until I finally got a Speed Graphic. A 3¼ x 4¼, and a flashgun, which was pretty damned heavy to lug up and down subway steps. But I was young then. It was during World War II, and even with money, you couldn't buy German cameras. Remember there were no Japanese cameras before and during the war. We were trying to kill as many Germans as we could, so naturally they weren't into selling us cameras then. In fact, *all* professional cameras were scarce. The reason I went to work in the nightclub as a photographer was only because the people who ran the concession also owned a photography store. That's how I eventually bought the Speed Graphic. Of course, that camera was very limited, but I did do a lot of publicity work. Then I bought my first 2¼ x 2¼. I was shooting the Fitzgeralds on television and they let me announce over the air that I wanted to buy a camera. Some listener came up with one. It was stolen in two weeks. The strap was cut when I was sitting in a coffee shop. Then I was an assistant for a photographer who was shooting a General Motors executive. He said he owned a camera he didn't need, and he sold it to me for $400. I don't know where I got the $400.

What kind of camera was that?

Rolleiflex. But I hated the Rolleiflex. I always wanted a 35mm. I was nearsighted and couldn't see the Rollei ground glass easily or focus properly. I couldn't walk with it while looking through the ground glass, or operate it with one hand. You can do all those things with a 35mm.

Anyway, I never felt competent with the Rollei. Then, in 1946, I spent the summer shooting at Tanglewood, and I made enough money—plus· $100 that a friend who ran the music store there loaned me—to buy my first 35mm camera, which was a Contax. From then on, it was ten times easier to take pictures that satisfied me. But, as you can see, it was a long hard struggle just to get a camera.

However, today I still don't have what I'd really like. Besides the Canonet, I have three Nikon bodies and three lenses. What I'd like is three to four compact bodies, plus five or six lenses.

I used to sell programs at the Hollywood Bowl when I was fifteen, just so that I could hear the music. So when I came to New York I'd go to Lewisohn Stadium just to listen to the New York Philharmonic rehearse in the daytime. I wanted to shoot pictures but all I had was the Speed Graphic at first. So there were two musicians who would sometimes loan me their cameras! Hoaever, on V-J night, Mayor La Guardia, of all people, was conducting the orchestra, and all I had was the Speed Graphic. Everybody was so happy. It was a fabulous way to celebrate V-J night . . . it was just a coincidence that he was conducting . . . but I didn't get anything I really liked.

When I finally bought the Contax in the fall of 1946 I double-exposed the first roll. But the second roll became my first double-page spread in *Look* magazine. I called it "Jimmy, the Storyteller." So it shows you, I needed the right camera.

What about some of the really high points in your career?

I think winning the *Life* contest was a nice validation. I remember the editor at *This Week* once saying, "Ruth can't take a single picture. All she can do is sequences." Well, I won third prize in the Individual Pictures division. I didn't lose in the other division, "Photo Essays," either. They gave "Jimmy, the Storyteller" Honorable Mention and published him as a double-page spread also, just like *Look*. To my knowledge, it's the only double-page spread that's been published in both *Life* and *Look*. I guess I have to thank my husband for that. He was the one who entered the contest for me when I was in Israel. I never would have entered "Jimmy."

Any other "ups" that you want to mention?

Well, I think the first Saturday that *The Little Fugitive* played, and we were very nervous. We went to see another movie on 57th Street, and I remember that I couldn't remember a thing about what that movie was about. We came out—the Normandy Theatre was on the same block—and we saw all those people on the sidewalk. We couldn't believe that they were standing in line waiting to see *The Little Fugitive*, and we got closer and closer, and there they were! Standing on line to see *our* movie. And here we'd knocked ourselves out for a year trying to get people to look at it free, at screenings.

At the beginning, it was the hardest thing to convince anybody, including our friends, that amateurs in New York had made a 35mm, feature-length fiction film that could compete with the Hollywood commercial product. It's very hard to, you know, blow your own horn. To try to convince experienced movie distributors that not all movies had to be made the Hollywood way. I don't know any other American who did it before us.

I have the feeling that you must have had to do that all your life to sell your pictures and movies. You had to blow your own horn.

I think there are very few successful photographers who probably haven't had to do the same thing.

Was the concept of doing movies yours, or was it between you and Morris?

Well, *Little Fugitive* was all Morris's idea. First he got a friend to build this special camera for him. It wouldn't have been possible without that camera. [Years later Jean-Luc Godard came to see it.] Then he got another friend to be his partner and help raise the money. Then he offered a professional film editor a percentage of the film. But at the first screening of the rushes, which I came along to see as Morris's girlfriend, the editor kept saying, "But Morris, where is Scene One and where is Scene Two?" Well, I was a magazine photographer, Morris was a magazine photographer. I knew exactly what he was doing and what was in his head. He was trying to make a fiction film around a simple story with candid material, and I thought it was great.

If you're going to start making movies without experience, what better background is there than being a magazine photographer who's worked for more than a week at a time (as we both had) on putting a photo essay together on a family, for instance?

However, at the beginning I kept telling him to make a short first and learn all the pitfalls, and his partner didn't want my assistance anyway, since I'd never cut any professional film, let alone a feature. However, as it turned out, there was not one filmmaker or professional film editor free in New York that summer who was willing to work for a percentage of the profits on a film that might never be distributed.

So that's how I became involved, first as the editor, and then as co-director. As it turned out, I had more knowledge than they thought I did. After all, I *had* worked as a messenger girl at MGM for six months! That may not seem like much, but apart from being the first girl messenger any studio ever hired, I was not your ordinary messenger girl. I was interested in "film." I had spent hours and hours in the Hollywood library reading every book that was ever written on filmmaking. In those days there were very few. You could do it. (Today it's incredible how much has been published about filmmaking.) Every day that I went to work, learning how they made movies is what kept my mind busy. Running messages I did on the side. So I felt perfectly equipped, in my amateurish way, for making *The Little Fugitive*. (I had even been invited by Orson Welles to watch him work at RKO after I wrote him a critical letter on *Citizen Kane*.)

When I was a little girl, people used to take their children to movies more. They didn't have baby-sitters. In fact, they even had a room for mothers with babies at the Grauman Egyptian Room on Hollywood

Boulevard. I remember being perturbed as to whether a scene was true to life, when I was four years old. I knew that it was acted, but I wanted to know whether it was true to life. I can remember that to this day. I wouldn't say that I wanted to make movies then, but I certainly was aware of them in a different way, I think, than somebody who just went to be entertained. I know I wanted to make movies when I was around ten years old when I went to the Saturday matinees and I'd see something that was really good, something moving.

You know, people have a certain feeling for certain things. Well, I feel that I always did for the movies. I was figuring out how they were made, where the cameraman was, what they went through to do this.

One of Morris's biggest strengths—and it is an unusual strength, I don't know anybody else who's got it—is that he can push the button on the camera . . . and remember it's not like taking a still picture, 'cause he doesn't know what's going to happen next . . . and things happen that are fabulous, just fabulous. When he said that he wanted to make movies by himself, after the first two, in one way I was extremely disappointed and depressed, and in another way I wasn't interested in working with anybody else unless they could shoot like that. I wouldn't have wanted to make a conventional movie then. I only wanted to make a movie that was filled with candid material, because I felt that was so exciting. Now I feel differently, of course.

Do you think that it is easier for a woman to break into photography now than when you did, considering that the whole field is very competitive now anyway?

No. For that reason. There is much more competition now from everybody, male and female. There are too many people who want to be photographers. In the first place, they think it is easy. I know, I've taught four classes. They just think it's a lot easier than it is. I think that one reason they want to get into it is because they think it is glamorous, and they think that you are going to get to meet a lot of famous people, and that it's fun to have your name in print, and they don't realize what you have to go through to get decent pictures. The wheedling, gate-crashing, salesmanship, the records, the collating and organization.

You were quoted as saying that when you teach people photography, you "try to teach them how to see." How can you really teach someone how to see?

I teach them how to isolate subjects, how to look. For example, we go out Easter Sunday and there's this fantastic mess of people. And you stand there and figure out how to isolate something that makes a picture by analyzing the light, the background, the activity.

Does this result in a Ruth Orkin school of photography?

I don't know. I don't think it makes any difference. First you have to come up with decent photographs. Then you have to figure the thing that makes them different from somebody else's. You can't have the teacher with you every minute, so you are going to be looking with your own eyes first, and then try to remember what somebody told you.

How did you learn to see?

My mother, probably. My mother had this scrapbook of pictures and she was fussy about what she put in, and then I remember going up big hills in cars and then looking at the "panoramic views." That was a phrase I knew at a very early age, "panoramic view." It was fun because it meant that you went on a drive up to Lookout Mountain and you saw a great view. Maybe some five-year-olds are not interested in great views, but they must have instilled it in me, because I can remember that as being a very nice memory. Not going on a picnic, not going to the beach, but going up into the mountains to see a panoramic view. So I think it has to do with your background.

Besides your books, what would you like to do?

I'd want to do movies that were truthful. The subject matter? I think that it's terribly immoral to force people to have children that they don't want. It's just so self-destructive of our society. I think that would be the main subject of any of my movies. I don't know how to get it all into words, even in my head, but I know how I feel. There just hasn't been enough done, and I feel that movies *should* have messages. There isn't enough time in the world for movies not to have messages, because too many people see them and they shouldn't be wasting their time, the way that most of them are. *And* there is no reason why it can't be the most exciting, interesting movie in the world and still have a message.

Eva
Rubinstein

Eva Rubinstein was born in Buenos Aires, Argentina, of Polish parents. She lived mostly in Paris until World War II, when she emigrated to the United States.

She attended Scripps College and the Theatre Department at the University of California at Los Angeles. She danced and acted on and off Broadway and on tour in Europe. She played in the original New York company of The Diary of Anne Frank for a year and a half. She has been married and divorced, and is the mother of three children.

Her photographic career began in 1968 with the help of Sean Kernan, and workshops with Lisette Model, Jim Hughes, Ken Heyman, and the late Diane Arbus.

Ms. Rubinstein photographs on two distinct levels. She does considerable free-lance work, chiefly editorial, documentary, and portraits, of very high merit. She also does much more private work: portraits, nudes, interiors, and her own special travel photos. Almost all of this work has been in black and white. Her eye is unique and highly sensitive.

She has been published in most of the major magazines, newspapers, and photographic publications in the United States, Europe, and South America. She has had numerous solo and group shows in the United States and abroad. She teaches in schools and photographic workshops.

Her one-woman shows have been seen at the Neikrug Gallery, New York City; La Photogalerie, Paris; Friends of Photography, Carmel, California; Gallery Trochenpresse, Berlin; Underground Gallery, New York City; The Dayton Art Institute, Ohio; Archetype Gallery, New Haven, Connecticut; The Washington Gallery of Photography; Frumkin Gallery, Chicago; and many others.

She has appeared in such group shows as "Creative Photography of the XXth Century" at Musée National d'Art Moderne; The Floating Foundation of Photography, New York; "Venus '71," Krakow, Poland; "America: Photographic Statements," Neikrug Gallery, New York City; "Critics' Choice," Neikrug Gallery; Salone Internationale Ciné Photo Optica, Milan, Italy; National Portrait Gallery, London; Fotografiska Museet, Stockholm, Sweden; and at least fifteen others.

Workshops she has conducted include the Ansel Adams Workshop in 35mm Photography (with Gary Winogrand), Yosemite, California; Photography Workshop at Arles Festival, Arles, France; Lightworks, Minneapolis, Minnesota; Maine Photographic Workshops; I.C.P. Advanced Weekend Workshop; Friends of Photography, Carmel, California; and University of Vermont, Burlington.

In 1974, Morgan and Morgan published a monograph of her photographs entitled Eva Rubinstein. A limited edition portfolio of twelve original prints was published by Neikrug Gallery in 1975. A slide/cassette module, "Eva Rubinstein Portfolio," has been published and is distributed by Photography Learning Systems.

Ms. Rubinstein's photographs hang in numerous private collections and in the Library of Congress; Metropolitan Museum of Art; International Center of Photography, New York; Bibliothèque Nationale, Paris; Musée Reattu, Arles, France; and Museum Sterckshof, Antwerp, Belgium.

How did you decide on photography as a career?

I got interested in photography the last year of my marriage, in 1967. I had been working part-time at a theatre. Someone who'd been an actor came back as a photographer. He was going to do their theatre photography. I got involved in helping him load cameras. Then he taught me how to print and I got absolutely, passionately bitten by it all.

I had been, before my marriage, an actress and a dancer, and even though I was fairly involved in those careers, I never felt as satisfied and fulfilled, and just completely overwhelmed by the thrill of doing something, as I was by photography. The strange ingredient that was so different about it was the matter of its lasting. It didn't just disappear overnight. Everything I had done before was ephemeral, it was gone in the morning. It gave me an incredible thrill to have something stay overnight. I had led a life where I worked and worked and worked, and two years later, who knew? Or the next day, who knew? There was nothing left of it.

Do you collect things?

Yes, I am a terrible, insane, inveterate keeper. It makes my life very difficult, because every time I have to move, I have piles and piles of things and scraps and letters and notes and memorabilia and God knows what kind of nonsense. I think it has a little bit to do with the fact that my family is European, and that a couple of wars wiped out all of the family stuff. Maybe that's part of it. It's like I'm collecting my own little family history. My poor kids will go crazy some day trying to sort it all.

I think that's why the photography meant so much to me. It was something of me that I could make into a material object. It is an expression of some part of my response to the world, my feelings about people, my vision of something, however minimal.

I've never had any illusions about being an artist. I don't think I am an artist. I don't create. I am a responder, I'm a reactor. That's what I feel about my work and about myself, as a person . . . sometimes a little too much so. I have a very hard time setting up things. I see them. I respond to them. I want to photograph them, people, things, whatever. I very seldom go out and set up something, create something. I just can't do that for myself. I wish I could because it would come in very handy in many situations on assignments. I'm not very good at it.

Why is that outside your definition of art?

Because I have a personal feeling that art has more to do with some kind of spontaneous combustion in your brain or something that is sort of born there. *Then* you make it materialize. You are a composer of music. You make the music in your head and then you put it down. You paint a painting which you have previously seen in your head, or do an interpretation, in paint, of something you have seen. Photography is a little different. The straight kind of photography that I do, which does not get involved in coloring or using negative images or double exposures or *any* of that, is at a different level. There *are* artist photographers whose work I would think of as art because, really, it is born in their heads before it is created on film. There are endless numbers of people who are artist photographers, or even artists who use the photographic medium as part of their art. Heinecken, for instance, uses printmaking, and uses collage and decoupage and photography, and drawing over it and painting over it and chalking over it—everything. Finally, he doesn't call himself a photographer. He says, "I am an artist." That is an artist. I may not always dig what he does. But he uses all kinds of media, and the pictures are born, pretty much, in his head, or "happen," in part, as he works.

I have a hard time even saying "I am a photographer." That is still a heavy sentence for me. So the idea of saying that I am an artist is probably more than I'll ever be able to say. Maybe I don't want the responsibility.

Could be. What *do* you say?

I say, "I photograph, I make photographs." Or sometimes I say, "I *try* to make photographs!"

Do you feel that you succeed in getting the image in the final print that you saw when you first took the picture?

When I first shot the picture, it was standing in front of me. It wasn't in my head. That's my point. I sometimes see "print" in terms of a print quality—whether it is going to be a dark picture or a light picture, or the things you have to sort of decide as you photograph, because you have to make the camera do it for you.

For instance, once I was in a room which was basically a white room flooded with sunlight. But I saw a dark picture in my head. So in a sense I translated a feeling I had about that room into darkness when there wasn't any darkness. So I exposed it so it would come out dark. The print is dark, and you don't see it as a light room, you see a dark room. That's just one of those strange things. It doesn't happen very often, but yes, sometimes I do see the print in my head before I take the picture.

Well, that makes you an artist at that point.

Well, again, I was reacting to some very strange vibrations in that particular room. It was the bedroom of some people I didn't know at all. The man I had never met, at the time, and the wife I had just met. I knew nothing about their lives, and then it turned out they were in the middle of getting divorced. So there may have been some strange thing in that bedroom that made me feel, perhaps, something dark.

Do you try to make any particular statement or statements with your work?

I can answer that almost in terms of what I try not to do. I prefer and I tend to make photographs that have . . . how to put it? If there is something negative in them, I try not to say something negative about the person in the photograph. I don't try to make mean ugly photographs of people, even if they sometimes look like mean, ugly people. I just try not to photograph them at all, unless they insist for some reason. Once or twice I photographed somebody I really didn't like, and the pictures came out looking very snide. I'd catch the person at a snide moment, and I didn't like those pictures very much. I'd almost prefer to just skip it. It doesn't give me pleasure to make a photograph which shows somebody being really unpleasant or ugly. I just don't like it. I don't get off on it any way at all.

I do prefer to see a moment where someone is being very much into himself, herself. When I was first doing portraits I was being very excitable and sort of manic. I was trying to get people to respond and look lively, and keep their eyes open and smile, etc. Slowly, as I got a little more confidence, I started almost backing away and getting more and more quiet, to the point where sometimes I would spend an hour with someone, and both of us would hardly be breathing, it would be so quiet. The click of the camera would be the only thing. I would barely whisper a thing, like, "Turn your head and look into the light," or just do it with my hand, indicating the direction, something, not to disturb the calm. And yet it was kind of a breathless calm, it was a very strange tension and calm at the same time. Now *that* is the way I prefer now to photograph people. In a sense, it allows them their share of the space between the photographer and the subject, and not the photographer taking up the whole space, and imposing his, her own desire, view, image, whatever. The other person is entitled to share in the image, and I like that.

Do you feel you succeed very often with this?

Sometimes. Sometimes I don't at all. I tend to succeed more when I photograph someone that I chose to photograph. Then the impulse on my part is enormous and whole. It's not that I am trying to photograph someone in order to please them, or a client, or a third party, or an art director, or anybody else. They haven't told me we need a vertical for this one and dramatic lighting for that one. I do what *I* feel, what I see, what I choose, and what I react to. Yet I am trying to make the person look as real, whole, good, as I can.

What kind of training have you had? Are you self-taught?

No. I started learning from the friend in Connecticut. He taught me printing and what a good print was. He showed me a lot of photographers' work. I simply had never been exposed to that entire world. I was totally thrilled by Harry Callahan. The first book I ever saw was called *The Photographer's Eye*. I liked Irving Penn portraits. I spent a lot of time emulating all of these people and then eventually tried to go off and develop my own way. A lot of my stuff is very linked to some of these people whom I have admired a great deal. They had a very strong effect on a lot of my work. August Sander, a German photographer who is dead now—his portraits of German people, before the First World War, between, and during the Second World War—he simply did a huge book, and it is the face of Germany. Everybody. Street urchins to the Gestapo. Actors, little town officials, people like that. Staggering, direct, wonderful photographs that show people presenting themselves the way they think they look best. There is something very touching and sometimes almost pathetic about their formality and about their seriousness. The quality of that just appealed to me enormously.

I was in a class given by Lisette Model. She was Austrian-born and lived in France and is a wonderful, white-haired fluff óf a woman. She looks like you could blow her away with a hard puff. She is one of the toughest people I have ever known in my life, and a wonderful teacher. Tough, abrasive, almost scary. It was during one of her classes that I saw that Sander book. She brought it in and it just knocked me out completely.

So I have had a lot of influences, and sort of indirect teaching, just from looking.

Do you do your own processing?

I started out doing everything. Then, five years into the game, I started making beginner's mistakes in film developing, so now I don't develop the film, which I basically don't enjoy doing anyway. I do make all my own prints of any work that I show in exhibits or sell. I do not do commercial printing on jobs that have to be published and have to be done in certain ways.

What basic equipment and film do you use?

I work with Nikons and Leicas. I had a Rollei 66 but it was stolen a couple of months ago, so I don't have that to worry about anymore. The film depends. If it's for me, privately, I use Tri X and Plus X for black and white, and whatever Kodak is putting out these days in terms of color. It changes a lot. On assignments I use whatever they ask for because it's up to them.

Do you do much color?

I don't shoot a lot of color for myself because I've only just recently begun seeing in color. I'm kind of interested to see what new turns my "seeing" will take, because it's been so heavily black and white until now. My own work, I mean, what I call my private work. I've started to see in color, and it's fascinating. It will be interesting to see what happens.

How much of your work is done on spec and how much on assignment?

Almost none on spec. I just don't like that very much. I do work on assignments and then I do totally my own. In other words, people and nudes, and places, interiors, whatever. Things that are *strictly* for me. And then maybe I'll have an exhibit or publication.

So I really have two different lives entirely, in the photographic field. I have an agent, Lee Gross, who is wonderful, and she deals with my annual reports and publicity photographs and newspapers and magazines and all that sort of thing. Then I'm connected with a gallery, Neikrug, which is also wonderful. She has charge of *my* own work, what I do for myself. She'll have another exhibit as soon as I am ready for it. Then she sends groups of shows out all over the country and all over the world. She does all the hard work, all the arranging and all the insuring. Then I sell prints through her. Each of these ladies makes 40 percent. Both of them happen to be very sympathetic, nice people, whom I like and get along with very well personally. They have both been extremely good to me. I mean, *really* good to me. I appreciate them enormously. When an agent finds me work that I never would have sought, on my own, obviously it's money in the bank.

Are there any assignments or types of assignments that you would not take?

I have turned down a few assignments where I just didn't feel I was qualified. I recommended friends who would be better. I would not go around pretending I can do something I don't think I can do.

I would also not do cigarette commercials, or something like that. There are some things I would not do in that sense. For either ethical reasons or moral reasons. I wouldn't do an ad for the Nazis.

I once accidentally found myself involved in a publication—it was really only the dummy of a publication—and they ran a portfolio of my photographs in this dummy issue. I then found out whose money was behind it and I almost had a heart attack. I was so mad. I just had them take my name off it, and I sent the money to a charitable organization which believed in precisely the opposite of what the backers would have liked. The funny part is, the thing ran without my name on it, and everybody knew whose pictures they were and kept asking me why my name wasn't on it. So when I could tell them the whole story, I was delighted.

Have you run into any particular problems as a woman in photography?

Yes. Weak shoulders. That is really the main problem. Simply the fact that I'm not as strong as a man physically, and I miss it desperately. It's very, very hard to carry things around. You do need a strong back. I think the fact that my Rollei was stolen . . . I think that God is slowly diminishing my heavy equipment.

I started in '68. I arrived at a moment where women were just beginning to be really almost sought after, in the sense of "Hire the handicapped." I saw lists in art directors' offices of women, and I would say, "What is this list of women?" And they would say, "Well, we decided that we haven't been hiring enough women and we're going to hire all these women." There was a real push for it. I'm not sure if I ever got or lost jobs, one way or the other, specifically because I was a woman, except for those few times when I knew they were looking for women because they hadn't hired any before.

But by now, and this is ten years later, as far as I know nobody seems to care much. If there are people who are not hired because they are women, I don't know about it.

Would you say at this point, disregarding how enormously competitive the whole field is, that a woman has as good a chance at making it in photography as a man starting out?

I would think so, yes. I have no reason to think otherwise, and I have no statistics. From what I hear, it is tough all over. It is incredibly competitive. Even the well-known people are not working a great deal. It's very hard. There are too many people. But what are you going to do?

You just started in 1968. This is only ten years now. You have done extremely well in ten years. Why? How did this come about?

I think that at the beginning, I absolutely worked *all* the time. I worked and worked and worked, and I pursued people to photograph them, and I took every trip that I could. I took every bit of money I could get and would go off and do trips and gather more faces and places and so forth. I was just immensely acquisitive. I was hungry, in a sense. I had just been divorced, I had left my family, and it was a very heavy time for me. It was very difficult. It just filled my life up, because I needed it filled up. Emotionally, there weren't too many other satisfactions at the time. It simply fulfilled the function of everything that was missing. That's why I worked so hard. So I think I simply did more work than someone else might have because it was a little compulsive. I was also being helped financially by my parents in terms of living expenses, so I could afford not to have to take a job in a studio or a lab. I did have some freedom to go out and do my own thing. Obviously, without that help I probably couldn't have done it.

The other thing is that I was a little older. I had been through twelve years of an extremely interesting and terribly difficult marriage, three children, and a rather complex home life with my own family before. Also a lot of traveling. A dancing and acting career on Broadway, and everything else. I wasn't just hatched. All the things that I was, whoever I was, got translated into another medium, to be expressed in a different way, which for me was very fulfilling. I could put everything into it. Even the dancing. I could get models to sit a certain way, show them how to do it. All that came in handy. Plus a certain amount of energy. It was just part of my life, all that. So it just went into another channel. If I had been eighteen or nineteen or twenty and just starting out, I might have had a whole lot less to say or feel. Instead of that, I was just totally into it. Everything I had went into it. I think that's why it happened sort of fast for me.

A lot of hard work and a lot of effort is what it boils down to.

Oh, wait a minute. Also a lot of luck, a lot of support, a lot of help. My friend who taught me certainly was a lot of support photographically. I simply couldn't have done it without the support. If I had had to be working at a nine-to-five job, in a lab, or holding lights for somebody else, I don't know if I could have. Then I was very lucky that I was getting positive response to my early work. I don't know what I would have done if I'd been getting negative response. I was extremely lucky that I was not put through that test.

When you sell your prints, do you sell them in limited editions?

Well, very early on when I sold prints I didn't pay much attention. I sold them myself, they cost $35, and I didn't exactly keep track a whole lot. But a few years later people started buying a little more seriously, and especially through galleries. I now number them and keep track of how many I sell, and make editions of fifty or seventy-five or one hundred. The Neikrug Gallery also sells them. At this particular instant, they are selling for between $125 and $150 through the gallery. I have one portfolio, twelve photographs in a box, which is out. The Metropolitan Museum has it. I have a little monograph which came out in 1975, published by Morgan and Morgan. That was terrific because it generated an enormous number of print sales. People are still ordering photographs from the book. Every time I have a show I get orders for prints through the galleries. That keeps coming in and it's very nice. What I need now, desperately, is to do some new work. Stop cooking and get back to photographing.

What is your goal?

I would enjoy very much being simply free to do my own work when I wanted to, have shows, sell prints, and then do my workshops and teaching. I like those very, very much. I use photographs the students do to try to get them to feel their own emotional *things* that are in their pictures. I don't teach *about* photography and I don't teach them to print better, unless they really want that. It gets much more, almost, into little encounter groups. It becomes like group leading, or just starting something going. Then the group starts being very supportive of itself. When that works at its best, it's very exciting. That really takes everything I've got. I love doing it.

Ideally, if I could survive financially on workshops, teaching, print selling, showing, etc., that would be very nice. But I'm afraid that is not realistic and the commercial work is something that I am committed to doing. To me it is more satisfying to do something for myself than to try and please a client, although I enjoy that also. It can be a challenge and it can be interesting and exciting sometimes. I am about to go down and do the official portrait of the Attorney General for the National Portrait Gallery, so that's rather exciting. It's an honor and it's a challenge, and it's kind of scary. It's not exactly an assignment, but it's kind of a neat thing.

That means carrying a lot of equipment down to Washington.

Well, I think I can afford an assistant on this one, which will be nice.

You do a lot of figure photography. What particular problems do you run into?

Well, one problem is that you don't really know what somebody looks like until they take their clothes off. Once they've got them off, and you don't really respond to the way the body looks or moves or something, it's very difficult to tell them to go home. It's much easier with faces because you can see them in advance.

I had a friend in Paris who was trying to do a nude in a certain way, and he said he had fifty-eight girls coming down the steps, and before they even reached the studio from the dressing room he knew that they were wrong, but he still had to go through an hour of shooting because he couldn't just send them home. That's happened to me half a dozen times.

Can't you interview the models beforehand, in the nude?

I don't use models very much. I just pick up people in the street or I meet friends, or friends of friends, or friends' kids, or a student in a workshop, whatever. It's fairly casual.

Way back when I started, I called models, but I can't remember when I last called a model for *me* to photograph. It's been a long time. Six or seven years. Occasionally I have to do it for the commercial work, but even that is very rare.

I really don't like that meat-market business of having people passing through and you look them up and down and say "yes" or "no," or "you're acceptable, you're not acceptable." It turns me off terribly, and it's one of the reasons that fashion photography doesn't appeal to me very much. I like to photograph people being who they really are. I don't even like photographing theatre, because you're photographing people being other people—actors. It was expected by a lot of people I knew, since I had been a dancer and an actress, that I would get into theatre photography. I didn't at all. I can't think of anything that turns me on less, because you are photographing somebody being somebody else.

Do you ever photograph people when they are being somebody else that they want to be?

Oh, of course. People are going to present you with some kind of a persona almost always, but the trick is to do it long enough. . . . Irving Penn once told me that he liked to peel people down like onions. He got very quiet and never had assistants around, and got them almost to be bored and tired to the point where their defenses were down, and then he would get the picture that was really good.

I am most interested in what people look like when they are all alone in their rooms. I try to recreate that, as much as is possible with a camera in the way, and another person, me, being there. I try to get that person to feel alone. To trust me enough to allow me to see them almost as if I weren't there. That's what I really like.

You mentioned a problem you once had with a nude model who would not let you publish his pictures.

That happened once. I took some pictures that I happened to think were terrific. Very, very real, expressive of him as a person. I was very pleased with them. I sent him the contact sheets, and he said, "Well, I don't know. I may have to run for senator some day." The likelihood of that is absolutely devastating. He had a rather large ego and was quite a silly young man. But, anyway, I was quite mad about that.

What happens is that you can't check somebody's body out until you see it. You can't ask a person to strip in the street just because you like his face. Sometimes you find that the faces don't go with the bodies and sort of contradict each other and don't match. So I spend a lot of time photographing bodies, or pieces of bodies, without the heads attached, because the two don't go together very well. In this particular situation I was especially mad because the young man's face went very well with his body, and it all worked together beautifully in the light and everything. It just pleased me enormously. Then he wouldn't let me use the stuff. I've been sort of looking to recreate that kind of situation again.

I was asked to do some male nudes recently for a show, and I simply didn't have time to do anything new. I had to put together some things from before, which again were headless. Right now I'm into a life where I'm much more involved with whole people. I would rather photograph a person who happens to have no clothes on, but still is a person, and has his or her own face, personality, and *everything else*. The next nudes I do . . . I will try everything possible to include faces and heads.

I've been pretty lucky about picking people up and not getting turned down too often when I want to photograph them. I find people on escalators and in phone booths and buses, things like that. Because I'm a woman—that's one of the times where it *is* handy—very few people feel that they are going to be threatened in any way. I have a card, and I have my name and stuff on it, and I say they can call me up, or check me out, or do anything they want to. They are much less apt to feel that I can harm them in any way. As a woman, that's one thing that works to my advantage.

If you were interviewing Eva Rubinstein, what questions would you ask that I haven't?

I would probably ask me something like, "What do you really think is important?" The one thing I would like to say has to do with those workshops. I found that the first couple of times that I was asked to teach, I felt like a fraud. I really didn't think I knew all that much about anything. What I found myself doing, eventually, toward the end of each group, was a one-to-one sort of thing with each person in the group. I'd look through their portfolios and talk to them very personally about what I felt in their work, and not in front of the other people. That seemed to be what worked best for everybody. That seemed to be what *I* could get into the most. At the next workshop I did, I was feeling in a very positive frame of mind at the time, and I suddenly found this enormous amount of energy and involvement in these people's work, as people—in the work as expressions of them as people rather than as photographs. And that's what started to happen. And I suddenly realized that I do photography because that is what happened with me. It fulfills whatever need I have to express whatever it is I have to express. I think what happens is that in the work one does, if you look at it all together, whether it's a few years or a lot of years or a lifetime, it's going to be a self-portrait. I think that's one of the reasons that I care a lot about how I photograph people. Because I see myself in all of those pictures. There is no way that they don't say more about me than they say about the person that I photographed. If I choose to respect somebody, that is a nicer statement about myself than if I am imposing something on somebody which is very nasty and ugly.

To show students that they are really telling a lot about themselves in a photograph that they take—it's almost like dreams—I always have them describe the photograph as though they were describing it to someone who is blind. They have to say *all* the things about the picture. I hate verbalizing about pictures, basically, but this has an entirely different purpose to it. The purpose is to show the person how much more of oneself there is in the photograph than they have ever known. They *really* get involved sometimes. It can get heavy. Sometimes you have to back off, because you get into such delicate areas.

This is where I find I have some kind of a little thing for leading them, when it is working and when I am being sensitive. On other days I just can't quite carry it off. To be totally sensitive to fifteen people at the same time, and feel undercurrents, and say, "She's not ready for this," or "He's not ready for that," or something, but it has to be said by one of the group members and not by me—all of that is not always possible. So it's extremely challenging, incredibly exciting, very moving to me. The students get very sensitized to themselves and to each other.

To develop the sense of trust among the group members, for each other, so that, say, the shyest person in the group is going to take *the* most perceptive portrait of one of the less pleasant members, an aggressive male or whatever, because her defenselessness would somehow take his defenses down. By the end of the week, some very terrific things have happened.

That's what I'm really interested in. What are people? What are we? How do we feel? How do we learn to speak with each other?

Bill Stettner

Bill Stettner was born in the Bronx, in New York City, thirty-nine years ago. His entire life has been influenced by photography; he was born the son of a photographer.

Mr. Stettner does both still life and illustration photography in his studio and on location. He is highly successful because his work is superb. Among his many clients he numbers the Reynolds Company, Phillip Morris, the Tobacco Institute, and Columbia Records.

He is on the board of the American Society of Magazine Photographers and is chairman of their Advertising Committee.

Mr. Stettner has received numerous awards, including several Andy Awards of Merit from the Advertising Club of New York, Art Directors Club Medals from the Art Directors Club of New York, and the International Broadcasting Award, honoring the World's Best Broadcast Advertisements, from the Hollywood Radio and Television Society. This last award was for one of the few films that Mr. Stettner has done.

The field of advertising photography is fiercely competitive. Although the elements needed for success are difficult to define, the following interview with Mr. Stettner points out many of them.

How did you get started in photography?

I have been in photography since I was eight, actually. My father was a photographer—candids, weddings, debutante parties, that kind of stuff. As a matter of fact, in '51 I did Bobby Kennedy's wedding pictures. I didn't even know I had them until he died. We worked for the bride's family. At that time they were the celebrities, to us. I was thirteen at the time.

I used to do all those bride and groom pictures. Used to go on Saturdays to the churches, do the pictures, and then run back and develop and print. That's how I started in photography. Then I went into the Navy in '57. I got switched to the photo department there, based on my photography background. In '59, when I came out of the service, my mother, who had been keeping my father's wedding business active, was disappointed that I wasn't going to continue with it. I began to do apprenticeship with guys like Maxwell Copeland, Dave Langley, Dick Stone, Arnold Newman, and others. I worked as an apprentice for five years. In '64 I went for a job and the guy said to me, "You can have the job, but your book is better than mine. Why don't you open your own studio?" He happened to be in the same building where a friend of mine was working, so I left that studio and went down and talked Buddy [John Paul] Endress into going into business with me. In '64 we opened a small studio.

We were partners from '64 to '70, at which time we split up, on good terms. At that time we were doing still life. He kept doing still life and I branched off into illustration. I probably now do 80 percent illustration, 20 percent still life.

So still life is not the big item, but you still do quite a bit of it.

Yes. What happens is that a lot of layouts involve a product shot as well as an illustration. Because I have a good still life background and my book shows that, my rep was able to capture a lot of jobs based on the fact that I could do both ends. He doesn't have to split up the job or go to two studios to do it. So it has proved an advantage in getting a lot of work which might have passed through the studio. I've been doing a lot of multiple-picture ads, involving some still life and some illustration. Phillip Morris and the Tobacco Institute are two of my clients. I do Camels—filters, regulars, and lights. I do those pack shots and cigarette pictures as well as the illustration.

I travel a great deal. I just spent two weeks in California. I was in Web City, Missouri. I was in Milwaukee for a week. I'm leaving for Las Vegas, and flying directly to Tucson. I'm back and I'm going to Cairo for two weeks for Camels, the Reynolds Company. Then I go to Louisville for Phillip Morris. And so I'm a traveling guy. I actually travel a little more than I like to.

Is that an enjoyable part of your work?

Well, I like the opportunity to see a lot of places on the expense account. Generally, the extended trips get to be heavy. The maximum I like to travel is two weeks.

What special problems do you run into with still life?

In a word, boredom. I do a lot of work for Columbia Records. I've been doing a lot of their platinum ads, which gives me the opportunity to do some really nice things. They're all concept ideas that are all photography, almost no copy, and I can get off doing those. I just frankly was offered some Seagram's V.O. work yesterday. It has those gold letters on the blue backgrounds, really boring. It was a guy I had been working for for a long time, and he called me and sort of hesitantly asked me if I would be interested in doing them, and I told him, in all honesty, that I would like to see him, and if that's the way I get to see him then I'll do the job, but I really don't have that much interest in it, if they're just those simple letters on the simple backgrounds. He said actually what he was hoping for was new ideas, something with maybe lightning bolts coming down, or some added piece of business. That kind of thing does excite me, the idea of a challenge. I've been working with the Camel Lights stuff and I've been using fiber optics. That too has been interesting. But generally I find that, after making a switch to illustration, and having the opportunity to do casting and location searching, just the idea of the logistics of the thing, the magnitude of the job, makes me like it a lot better. The truth is, it consumes a lot more time and it isn't as financially rewarding as still life was. I feel I can do three or four still lifes a day, if I had to, whereas in illustration the time is pretty rigid. Models, booking, location necessitate you being there at a certain time, whereas with still life you have the flexibility of changing your schedule. You can do what you want to do when you want to do it. I find there is good and bad to both, and I feel like right now I'm riding a crest, I'm really busy, things are really good. I've been around now fifteen years. People know who I am. I'm hearing from guys I haven't heard from in years, who have made the rounds and tried a lot of other photographers and have now come back.

When you do special effects work—you talked about fiber optics and so forth—who pays for the gear?

They pay for everything. For everything. I have my standard allotment of equipment. I've got Nikons and Hasselblads and Deardorffs. I have a full complement of lenses and strobes, and whatever any normal job would call for. When it came to fiber optics it was something that I had never played with. Other guys had done work on the account before me, and I have relationships with a lot of photographers. I'm on the board of ASMP, I'm chairman of the advertising committee, I know pretty much everybody in commercial photography in New York. In this case both Michael O'Neil and Buddy Endress had worked on Camel Lights, and had experience with fiber optics. So when I was given the project, I did what I considered to be the obvious thing, and that was to call both those guys and pump them. As a matter of fact, I went up to Buddy's studio and he recreated the set for me and showed me exactly how it was done. From there, I improved on it. I searched for better fiber optics, something that would transport more light, something that would work better.

My inexperience was overcome by my questioning my peers. I feel I would never ask anybody for anything I wouldn't give them or haven't given them in the past. Guys call here all the time. Particularly since I am the chairman of the advertising committee for ASMP. I would say in the last three months I've heard from Pete Turner, Henry Sandbank, Allen Vogel. They all called with their problems. And I return their questions to ASMP, to the board, and to my advertising committee, and we see if we can't come up with answers.

Right now we've reached the point, and I think we're operating with about ninety percent effectiveness, where we get film and processing on every job, at every agency, and up until January of this year that was not the case. Some guys got it, some guys didn't. If you knew how to get it, or if you were in a position to demand it, you would get it. Other guys didn't. We sent directives to the agencies saying that anyone who uses an ASMP photographer will pay film and processing. They still have resisted it. A lot of guys have given in and have taken it off their bills, or billed without it, based on the premise that they don't pay it. However, it's their loss, because the agencies are paying it.

For your still life work, do you use anything but strobes?

100 percent. Since '64 I've been using the strobes. Bernie Gold probably taught me the most of any of the guys I worked for. He's probably the least known of all the guys I worked for and probably taught me the most. He was, and is, a tungsten expert, but around that period of 1959 or '60, strobe was not very popular, and he was a master at incandescent lighting.

Which films do you use?

I use Tri X for black and white. I use Ektachrome 8 x 10, and Kodachrome 25 is the one I like in color for 35. I've tried lots of other films and had a lot of bad experiences. Since we've gotten over the trauma of the disappearance of Kodachrome II, I feel like I've found a certain amount of safety in Kodachrome 25. I'm one of the few guys around that does not bracket. I don't have the patience for bracketing. I can't take the same picture thirty times. I'm nervous waiting for the film to come back. When I'm shooting I can get excited, but when I have to bracket, I can't shoot. It clouds my head.

Do you do any of your own processing work?

I have all the color processing done outside, 100 percent.

How competitive is your business?

It's fierce. It's fierce. However, I believe there's enough for everybody. And I believe that even when I don't have work. I always blame it on my rep. While the competition is fierce—there are 1200, 1500 commercial photographers in New York City—there is enough work for everybody. I've been in business fifteen years and I've always made a good living. Sometimes better than others, but always done well. I feel like the work is out there and there is a remarkable amount of markets that guys don't have any awareness of. I keep saying ASMP, but I have been quite active there over the past four years and instrumental in bringing advertising photographers into ASMP.

Collectively, the advertising committee and guys like myself who worked at it brought in some 650 advertising photographers. They now, in effect, control a good portion of ASMP, and have turned ASMP around from magazine and reportage guys to a great deal of advertising photographers. So we do have a camaraderie and a closeness and I feel like it has opened up a good rapport among photographers. Where guys were secretive before, kept very much to themselves, now I think you will find there are lots of photographers who are friends, which is something I have seen evolve in twenty years in this business.

How difficult do you think it would be for a young, talented, new photographer to break into the business?

It's tough. It's really tough.

You work, pretty much, with a rep?

I believe in representation, I'm a *strong* believer in representation. As recently as yesterday, my rep was up at Doyle-Dane. She sees a guy, she says, "How you doin', how come we don't hear from you?" He says, ". . . how come you don't hear from me? How come Bill never calls me to say hello?" It's that contact, it's that connection to the people out there. You are only as good as the moment that they're with you. It takes her a long time, many appearances, to wrap up a job. And then the guy will come down here, and maybe I'll have a two-hour period with him, at which time I'm working and distracted by the job. I don't have much time to build a relationship with the guy. And that's where repeat business is at. Delivering a good job and developing some rapport with an art director. And in that limited period it is difficult to do it. And guys feel they want to have a working relationship with somebody. They want to have personal contact with them. I feel that that's the function of a rep. It's beyond going out there, showing my portfolio, and ripping a layout out of his hands. It's selling him. She travels very often without a portfolio, just doing how-de-do's, you know?

What percentage base do most reps work on?

Well, a standard in the industry is 25 percent. Many guys today are getting off the percentage basis and getting on to salaried people. I can think of three guys right offhand that always had representation and have now turned completely around. They now have a salaried person who carries their book around. They don't pay commission. They feel that their reputation is enough to keep them busy, that the phone will ring and then all they have to do is send somebody up to pick up a layout. I personally don't believe in that. I believe that that contact is essential. I have looked long and hard, I've had many reps over the years, and I've had a *few* that I've had really good working relationships with, those who have not been greedy, who have proved themselves to the point where I feel they have earned a percentage of my business. I'm a *firm* believer in representation.

I have exclusive representation, but a lot of reps represent, say, three photographers. Reps can, in fact, make more than photographers. They have no capital investment, no vested interest. They come in and immediately demand 25 percent of the gross fee. With just three successful photographers doing a minimum of $250,000 billing, we're talking a $200,000 gross income for a representative whose expenses probably come to $20,000 or $25,000 over the year, which makes it a neat net.

Do you get a lot of people coming in for positions?

Yes. Right now I happen to be looking for a studio manager. I'm having trouble finding one. I've spoken to twelve or fifteen guys since the word hit the street that I am looking. A lot of guys have called. None have the experience I am looking for. I need somebody who has three years of comparable experience, who has run a studio, who has had to pack, do logistics, and order supplies.

Do you ever take on inexperienced assistants?

I do. I have three assistants. My studio manager is a heavy, minimum three years experience, a guy who is getting ready to go into his own business. I don't hire professional assistants. I like a guy who has learning interests and who has the energy and potential to open his own studio and be a photographer, although he doesn't do any photography for me per se. I do all the photography myself. I like a guy who has plans, who is here to learn as much as he can, and at the same time build a portfolio. Maybe this is his last job before he opens his own studio. Then I have a first assistant, who is a guy who is a decent printer, and can take a little direction, and improve some of his skills. Someone who can stand by and cover anything my studio manager is too busy to do. Then I have a second assistant, who is kind of a go-fer, and a guy who does the basic developing and contact printing and stuff like that, who generally moves up to the next spot when it opens, depending on his readiness. Right now I have second and first assistants. My first assistant is not ready to move up to studio manager, so I have to hire over. I *always* prefer to take my next guy in line if I can. The third guy in line usually is some guy who has a high interest in photography who will work very cheaply for the experience.

This sounds like something out of your own background.

Absolutely. I believe it has held me in good stead. I worked in a lot of studios. I stayed as long as I felt I was learning something. The minute I felt I wasn't learning anymore—it didn't have anything to do with money, my prime interest was education—I moved on. When I reached the position where I had worked for enough guys, and felt competent that I could handle any job, I struck out on my own. However, I learned rather quickly that I couldn't handle any job. It took several years of being in business before I had the feeling of confidence, and then I wasn't threatened by any job that came in. There have been *very* few jobs over the years that I wasn't able to accomplish through experience or advice from my peers. So I didn't anticipate any anxiety over any assignment that I received in the last five years, anyway.

Would you care to make any comments on formal teaching of photography?

Yeah. I'm anti-school, frankly. I feel like many of the schools still spend a good portion of the time on such wasted things, things that have no relation to the actual business. Like chemistry. I'm in business fifteen years and I never mixed a single chemical with the exception of hypo, which is just nothing except crystals and some water. To spend time on chemistry is absurd. There are a lot of things that I know from school, and from some guys that I've worked for. In the old days, guys did mix their own chemicals, and that stuff was important, but today everything is premixed, prepackaged, and you don't have to know that stuff. I think it is a waste of energy. It doesn't apply to commercial photography. Even a guy who is out in the field taking pictures of wrens copulating, for *National Geographic*—I don't know why he has to worry about the chemistry. He's not developing his film. He'd rather sit in the field and watch the birds. He sends it out to a lab and hopes they know what they are doing.

You have, nevertheless, obviously developed a tremendous feel for the mechanics of the craft, including the films and what can be done, just from your experience.

Yeah. It comes from experience. I've had a lot of guys here who have come out of school and accepted the bottom position in the chain and, after six months of on-the-job training, have appreciated that in six months they have learned far more than they did in three or four years of school, and they feel that while school helped them a little, it certainly was a waste of time, by their own admission. I have no prejudice against guys who have gone to school. However, I would just as soon pick a guy who had six months on-the-job training as a guy who had four years of school. I am a firm believer in apprenticeship. I try to operate the studio on that premise. I want to have the guys here who want to learn. It has nothing to do with money. I'm a tough boss, and while my staff will say "Whew, he can really drive you," they'll also say that I am fair and honest and that they have all learned something. Very often they don't realize what they've learned until they go to somebody else's studio. Then the guy will call me back and say, "I can't believe it, my boss was knocked over by how much I knew. And it's stuff that I learned being with you, by you busting my chops and making me make another print even though I thought it was all right."

Do you ever do any shooting for your own pleasure? Do you carry a camera around?

It's rare. Rare. I carry an EL and I noticed this year that I spent more than the cost of the camera in repairs on it. So I just stopped carrying it. For the two rolls of film that I put through it in the last year for personal things . . . it's like the shoemaker's son going barefoot. I don't have a picture of my six-year-old son since he was four and a half.

I like photography, I like what I'm doing. I can sit for hours and talk with art directors about advertising. I have a good time. I put in so many hours here. Now I'm going to Arizona with some friends for a week. Obviously, I'm going to bring my cameras, as I've done in the past on any vacation that I've managed to grab. However, if I took six rolls of film in six vacations, I took a lot. Most of those are pictures of my wife or my kid, or the people we were with.

What gives you the most satisfaction, the results you end up with or the process of creating them?

Well, the results don't always meet my expectations. I have a tremendously high energy level while I am shooting. I get tremendously turned on. And I like to shoot. And very often, what I see in my mind's eye comes back on the film. As I said before, when it reaches the stage of reproduction, when I turn the pages of the magazines and see my pictures, I get off. I like riding down the highway and seeing *my* billboard. That still turns me on, some fifteen years later. However, the disappointments—what the clients do with what I do—have sort of turned me off. I don't look through the magazines like I used to. When the magazines came, before I looked at the checks or the mail I looked through the magazines to see what I had in there. Today I turn pages a lot, I keep track of who does what, I know what most of the guys in town are doing and who's working on what account, by reading the trades. I keep close watch on the trades. I keep close watch on which art directors are where and who's doing what. I feel like this is a business, not an art. Guys who come out of school and think they are artists are in for a gross surprise if they choose to go into commercial photography. There are a lot of opportunities for reportage photography, but you can't make a living doing that, I don't believe. You've got to do it for love. And, frankly, it was the high-income possibilities that got me interested in this business.

Do you often get the picture you see in your head, or do you more often get something that is not as good as what you had visualized? Looking back at photos taken several years before, do they get better with age?

I would say very often that's the case. I like to think that I can get what I see in my mind's eye on film. It's not as easy as it appears. Given all the budget in the world, you can't always get it down on film the way you see it in your mind's eye. And I'll tell you that my most famous photograph is the flag made out of matches. It's probably one of *the* most famous photographs in the history of commercial photography. I have used it time and again as my logo. However, I did that as a sample from an idea that just came to me one night, as I was sitting around looking at a pile of "strike-anywhere" matches. It looked like a field of the flag. It was done in 1970 and when I did it, my rep fell on the floor. He said it's the best picture he ever saw and how terrific it was going to be, and how it was going to make me famous, and . . . well, I thought, what a shmuck he was. As it happens, it turns out he was right. It wasn't until a year and a half after I did it that I appreciated it.

That's fascinating. That was a picture that was done for your own pleasure?

Yeah. Well, actually it wasn't for my own pleasure. It was done under duress. The idea was mine, the concept was mine, and it was at a point where I had just split up with my partner and felt I had to build a new book, so I had to do samples. And that's how that came about. It wasn't out of a desire to do fresh pictures, frankly, it was out of necessity.

Do you still do any sample shots?

On a rare occasion I do. It's tough, though, to get into gear. However, when art director associates suggest that they would like something for their portfolio, an experimental thing for a client, I do like to do that. I feel like there is less control. I can almost deliver it and be sure he is going to like it. When I am working in an experimental area as opposed to a specific assignment for bucks.

If you were conducting this interview, what questions would you ask yourself that we haven't covered?

I would maybe ask, "What is the best advice you could give to somebody who was interested in becoming a commercial photographer?"

I feel like I was one of the best assistants there ever was. I feel like when I accepted a job, I did the best I could. I never considered what I was being paid or what I was working on, or who I was working for. I always treated a job as a lesson. I always gave whoever I worked for the best I could give them, and I feel like some guys appreciated it, some didn't. Some could afford to pay me more, for working hard, and some couldn't. But, I always turned to. I always feel like that is what I look for in an assistant. The guy who's got the high energy level to devote all his time and give up his personal life. . . . I sound like a slavemaster to myself, but I really believe in the guy who has a sincere interest in photography and works hard at it, and not only on things that I give him to do, but on assignments that he gives himself.

I have had, over the last fifteen years, I'm embarrassed to say, probably a hundred assistants, and very few of them are in business for themselves today. And very few of them, an *amazingly* few of them, have taken advantage of the prime opportunity of using *my* studio, *my* facilities, *my* equipment, and *my* supplies, as a matter of fact, to build their own portfolios. And I tell you that I could put a record up which would say "You have the opportunity to do all that while you're here. Don't wait till you go out on your own to build a book. You are going to blow a year out there, and that can be a very expensive year. You can start earning immediately if you prepare a portfolio while you are on the job, and once you have your book, you then start out on your own studio. You don't leave a job and then begin to do samples." And it's just a flimsy excuse to say that you just don't have the time to do your own stuff when you are working for somebody else. That's the *prime* time to prepare for going into business on your own—while you are working for somebody else. And I tell you there are a lot of my assistants who have attempted to go into business with that attitude. "I'm going to do samples, I'm going to open a studio, and I'm going to keep expenses down. I'm going to do samples, and hopefully I'll get enough small jobs to keep me going." Well, that year they managed to save enough money to get through, but it takes a long time to build a portfolio. Now I am here fifteen years and I'm learning from some really big clients with big budgets, and there isn't a guy out there who can top my pictures without those advantages. Well, there aren't *too* many guys out there, let's put it that way. And so I've seen the studios open and close. My advice is, get the portfolio before you open a studio.

Donald
Strayer

In newspaper photography, more photos are printed than in any other area of the field. They are seldom carefully planned and artistically executed, but they reach a huge market. Some photographers go in and out of this field. Others spend their whole professional lives in it. Some are simply doing a job, but some take pride in their work and produce consistently good photos in a field not generally known for its sensitivity and artistry. Award-winning photographer Don Strayer is one of those few.

Mr. Strayer has spent all his news years on the staff of the Toledo Blade, one of the finest newspapers, not only in Ohio, but in midwestern America. He was born in 1934 in Grand Rapids, Ohio, at the north end of Wapakaneta Road. Wapakaneta Road also produced another famed Ohioan when the first man to walk on the moon, Neil Armstrong, was born at the south end, not too much later than Mr. Strayer.

He is a self-taught photographer, a graduate of Bowling Green State University, and the father of a twenty-two-year-old son, Larry. He shoots skeet and archery at a Toledo conservation club, jogs, bicycles, and can be found on cross-country skis in the winter. Most of the time, he has a camera with him.

How about some general background on how you work at the Toledo Blade?

The *Blade* is a large newspaper covering all of northwestern Ohio and southwestern Michigan. The newspaper covers this by having several different departments, or "desks."

The biggest desk is the national desk. They take all their photographs from wire photos, which is an old term. Now they are called laser photos. The *Blade* uses A.P. [Associated Press]. Then there is the city desk, which covers Toledo proper, plus close outlying areas. The regional desk covers the rest of the territory, anywhere else in the state or lower Michigan.

We have four editions. The first one comes out at 8:30 in the morning. It is what we call the three-star, or regional, newspaper. This is the one that goes out to all the farms and little towns. Then there are two editions in the early afternoon, one about one o'clock and a remake at 2:30 to 3:00 P.M. These are for home delivery. The final edition, at 4:00 P.M. is the Blue Streak edition. It has the stock closings and all the latest news.

There are other "desks" within the newspaper, such as "Living Today" or the women's department. There is a religion page. There is the Sunday department, which works basically for the Sunday paper, but they are also in charge of putting out special editions.

There is only one photo department, and it has about twelve people. These twelve people work about eight hours per day, Monday through Saturday. The first photographer comes in at 7:00 A.M., the next one at 8:00, and then two or three will be in at 8:30. They are off after 7¾ hours of work. Then one comes in at 12:30, one at 1:30, and one at 2:30. So someone is generally in the photo department from 7:00 A.M. to 11:00 P.M. Anything else that happens, such as a disaster, would be covered by a photographer who would be called at home and go out on overtime. This very seldom happens. We don't chase all accidents or fires. If a second or third alarm is called in, then we go see what it is all about. The *Blade* is not a sensationalist newspaper. But this does not mean that they don't want to see the pictures. Many times the editors want to see the pictures to determine whether or not they should print them.

Let me get into a little bit more about my work. I go in, for instance, at 8:30. When I get in, I may have an assignment right away, or there may be nothing for an hour or two. Maybe the assignment comes from city desk. In that case I'll have to go out and cover the mayor, or someone who is protesting something, or some person who has just made a long bike trip. I never know. Many times they will give me an assignment slip and send me out to cover three or four jobs. Most of the time I work alone, just myself and my car. Many times I have to accompany a reporter. The photographers have the cars. We pick up the reporters, take them out, listen to the story that they are taking, get the pictures, and then bring the reporters back and get the pictures off. Sometimes we may just bring the reporters back, or even send them back in a cab and go on to another assignment.

Most of the time we do not know what the reporter wants. You have to stop, ask the people what the reporter talked about, and then get your picture or pictures. Sometimes it's a simple one-picture job. The next time you may have eight or ten pictures.

Once I get my assignments, take the pictures, and get back to the photo department, then I have to process the film. Almost all the film is black and white. We do color work, but we do it for the Sunday department. They generally use only color covers. So if they cover four stories in the Sunday magazine, only one will have a color photo, on the cover.

We generally use Kodak's Tri X, and we print on DuPont or Kodak paper. I prefer Polycontrast paper, just because it's the one I generally work with and know. In newspaper work, we do have some help from an art department. The artists retouch pictures, many times taking out distracting signs. We give the desk that we are working for a picture that may need some work. It may have some extra space around it. The editors will chop down the picture to the size or content that they want.

We don't have a lot of secrets that we use in the darkroom. We dodge and burn in. We use potassium ferrocyanide for bleaching. That's about the extent.

Just to get an idea of your actual working schedule, would you care to review several recent days?

On the first of June, I spent an hour or two just copying old books from the public library for a slide presentation to show how Toledo has changed over the last one hundred years. That was two 36-exposure rolls of film. Then I went to a local public television station for a school tour. Then I ended up at Anderson's grain elevators, where they are building five new grain storage tanks. One of these pictures was for Associated Press, for an article on grain shipments, etc. That was the end of that day. Two rolls of color film were shot. Channel 30—the school tour—was three pictures turned in, one used. On the grain elevator I shot a roll of film, forty exposures. I made four prints, and one picture was used with the story.

Then I was off until the sixth. Then I went out with the food editor to do a story on how they had changed an A & P grocery store into a restaurant. A one-picture assignment of the waitresses holding the eight house specialties. From there I went to St. Mary's at Rosford to shoot Coach "Digger" Phelps. Then out to the Northwood No. One Fire Station, where they wanted ten different pictures for a special fire edition. The firemen of northwest Ohio were having a three-day convention, or beer blast.

The next day a one-picture of a golden wedding anniversary, then a little girl who was a Cappy Dick winner, then to No. Two Northwood Fire Station for ten more pictures. Firemen with the Rescue Squad, firemen with twenty-five years service or more, the whole department, this new fire truck, that new fire truck, etc., etc. Out of the total of twenty pictures, they will use eight in the special edition.

The next night I did a head shot of a man at the YMCA. Then the assistant to the head of HUD on a tour of Toledo. I had to follow him around town. Then back out to Northwood High School, where three of the firemen were decorating the high school for the convention. Then out to Perrysburg for a shot of four teachers retiring from Perrysburg High School.

The next night I was out at Anderson's office again, this time to shoot the Andersons for a special Father's Day edition on Sunday. From there I went out to Camp Palmer and shot eight pictures of 4-Hers with their horses. Sounds exciting, huh? There were eight pictures taken; five will be used.

Saturday night was quite free. I ended up roving for early news, which took me all over the city looking for different things happening to fill in for Sunday's paper.

Sunday I was off. Monday I went in at 2:30 and the first thing I did was go to Elmore for Weather Art. We had a drive-in movie screen blown over and from there we went to shoot pictures of an old fellow's trailer that had the roof blown off. Then I ran out to Lakeside, Ohio, where the Methodist

Church was having a week-long convention. I shot twelve pictures. We used two or three on Tuesday, and from then on we used one for the regional desk and a different one for the area edition, every day, for the rest of the week.

On the thirteenth, I came in and started doing some printing. A new experimental ship, a Canadian ocean-going vessel, ran into the Cherry Street Bridge. It had loaded and was leaving to go out to the Lake Erie channels. The bridge was stuck open for two hours. I had to drive "around" the river on another bridge. Got on board with the Coast Guard, went out, took pictures of the ship, and then rode up with them to shoot the damage to the bridge. I shot a roll of film plus five or six more exposures. I made four prints and two got into the paper. After that I spent the rest of the evening in the Safety Building shooting pictures of a home raffle, where they give away old homes in depressed areas if you move in and improve them. They figure it's cheaper to do that than for the city to demolish them, and it is an attempt to get people to move back into the city.

That's certainly a variety of assignments in eight days. What effect does a photograph have on the readership of a particular story?

Any picture which appears in the paper automatically increases readership of that story. If it is on the front page, readership is about 80 percent with a picture. If it is on the inside, readership will go down to 60 percent with a picture, and 30 to 40 per cent without a picture. The farther you get back into the paper, the lower the readership, but it will still be increased with a picture.

How did you start in photography? What was your training?

I started photography in the sixth grade. It was all self-taught. I borrowed a *lot* of money, $180, from Grandma, to buy an old Speed Graphic and a complete darkroom outfit, and from there I guess I was rather lucky. I would do pictures of Boy Scout trips, I would do pictures for the yearbooks, I would do pictures of people for the school newspaper, and people seemed to like it.

Wanting to go to college, I decided to go into the Army, to get the G.I. Bill. I was trained as a clerk-typist and sent to West Virginia. As usual, I ended up doing photography. We had a darkroom and a photographer. He was married, so he wanted me to help him. So I got a little bit of on-the-job training in the Army.

When I returned, I went to Bowling Green State University, starting in pre-med. Money-wise, again, I transferred to education, decided that wasn't for me, and ended up with a liberal arts education. When I got out I started working at the *Blade*. I was also working at a camera store, and had gotten married.

My education has really been picked up from the library, from books, from on-the-job training, and so forth. As an example, one day I was in the museum shooting an assignment for the paper. I heard a volunteer talking about one of the paintings. I found there was a wealth of information that this art teacher gave me. I've found that almost anything you take in life is going to help you one way or another. Everything can be used in your photography. You are working with physics and chemistry when you are working with basic photography. In the news field, you are working with people, and this is the fascinating part. Many people forget that these people *are* people, and they have different ideas, and any training you have will help you in interacting with them, in getting a better picture, many times. Of course, sometimes it doesn't make any difference.

There has been a lot of fun, a lot of laughter, I've done a lot of things. You've got to understand, each day when I go into work, I have *no* idea what I am going to do. Anything that can be happening in the news, I may cover.

Do you think that photography can actually be taught on a formal basis?

I'd have to answer yes, Jerry. Ohio University at Athens, Ohio, has two types of photo courses. They teach photography as an art form. They're very good at it. We have had photographers come from there, go to the *Blade*, get into the news business, and be very good at the news business, even though their hearts were in the artistic part of photography. Today they have one of *the* best instructors in journalistic photography. When I see editors take these kids, and have them end up as photographer of the year in the state, as news photographers, or winning all sorts of awards where news photographers compete, I would have to say that there are certain people who *can* teach photography.

When did you decide to make your living as a photographer?

Photography was always something that I enjoyed. Even in pre-med, I would often become extremely tired, at two o'clock in the morning, and if I would pick up something on photography and read it, for sometimes only ten minutes, it was a change of pace that would revive me. I would have to say that in 1960, when I went to the *Blade* as an intern, I decided that I liked the field. But then, as I said, I got married, we had a child. . . . Do you get stuck? Do you get caught in a place? I'm trying to figure that out now.

Do you do work other than newspaper photography? Do you do commercial work?

I do some commercial work for magazines. All of us do, I suppose. You do it basically because it adds a little bit of money, but I think there is another drive. If you are interested in photography, you always like to see your work published. You like to see it in the newspaper you work for, you like to see a by-line, and therefore if you do work for a magazine or another newspaper, you are always curious to see what *they* do with your work. As a news photographer, you don't have a lot to say about what they use in the paper and how they use it. So I think there is always that desire to see what someone else would do with your work. We don't make a big thing out of it, and the *Blade* doesn't like to have you do it, but you do it because you want to see what they can do with your work.

I found that even *National Geographic* photographers conform to the style of the magazine, after they are there for a short time. Now many of them, after they shoot for a while, are so radical that even the older editors will change their opinions and adopt the photographer's type of work. Over ten or twenty years a magazine or newspaper will change its format because of the type of work the photographers are doing for them. It's the same old story. Photographers do have to bend to shoot for their publication, and editors find that after a while, more and more photographers are going to a different style, so. . . . Why did the old 4 x 5 give out? If editors had had their way, we never would have gotten away from the old 4 x 5 format. Younger photographers, when I first came to the *Blade*, just made the older photographers keep up so much, because we were using 35mm and they were using 4 x 5s. Eventually, the editors came to the older men and said, "Hey, why can't you do this? Why can they do that?" It's a give-and-take situation.

Do you do any shooting for your own pleasure?

I'll have to admit that I love nature work. I love doing different pictures. In bicycle work, in cross-country skiing, in my jogging. Because the *Blade* does essentially all black and white work, I find that I end up doing color work for myself. Every once in a while I can do something and it ends up in the *Blade* Sunday magazine in color.

What awards have you won?

Ohio News Photographers is a state organization for press photographers. Then there is National Press Photographers. I belong to both. I've won awards from both, but mostly the state organization. To crack the awards in the National is pretty hard. I've often thought of sitting down and studying, and seeing if there is a way that you can work the field to win awards. After you have worked for a long time you get to know the judges and you can work the state, although I don't try as much as I used to.

Discuss the equipment you use and how it has changed over the years. What changes do you expect or would you like to see in the future?

I carry one camera, a Nikon F-2, a small strobe outfit, and about four lenses. Many of the people at the *Blade* now are starting to carry the smaller Nikon FMs or the Nikkormats. The lenses we carry are either a 21mm or 24mm (I use a 24), a 35mm, which is a little faster with an f 2 lens, for available-light work. I don't carry a 50mm. I don't even have one now. We have an equipment locker where we have long lenses and fisheye lenses. We have up to 500mm telephotos. The other two lenses that we carry most of the time are 105mm, used for portraits and close work, and a 200mm.

I have two camera bodies, but I generally only carry one. The other one is usually locked in the car somewhere, so that if I have trouble with my camera, I can get at it.

We have used flashbulbs until the last year or two, simply because we get better synch with flashbulbs. The strobe will only synch up to 1/125th of a second. We also get more light out of the flashbulbs. I use a Vivitar 283 automatic strobe, and I really like it. I can balance this so it overexposes or underexposes. Basically, I use it about a stop under, as fill light, and still shoot available light. It gives you that extra little kicker under the eyes, and so forth.

I also carry a tripod but don't use it too often. We do have quartz lights that we take out for color work, and larger strobes when we need more light, but most of this is kept in the equipment locker.

The *Blade* has gone electronic. Not photographically, but with most of our printing. They've cut the back rooms out. They've gotten rid of the linotype machines and all that. I look for only a short time before newspaper photography goes electronic.

What special pressures do you operate under as a news photographer?

Pressure. Boy, that's the name of the job. We don't have the pressures that we used to, when we had three or four deadlines a day. But it seems like everything you shoot is for the same or next day, so everything you shoot has got to be processed and gotten out. Many times I will go in at 8:30 in the morning, have to drive out ten, twenty minutes, shoot a picture, drive back, and get it in by ten o'clock. Well, that's an hour and a half. I believe the record is: I have gone into the darkroom, literally *cut* the film out of the camera, processed for three minutes, fixed for thirty seconds, washed for thirty seconds, printed the film wet, in the enlarger, and I think about 6½ minutes is the record for walking in the darkroom and walking out with a dry print for city desk. That's pretty fast, but we do it. Any faster and the print would be turning yellow in your hands because it hadn't been fixed or washed long enough.

What assignments do you enjoy most?

I think a photographer has to be versatile, particularly if he is working for a newspaper. I think that's why I don't get tired of this job, because of the variety. I do think that if I had to do all one type of assignment I'd grow tired of it.

Several years ago they opened the Cleveland Coliseum, and Frank Sinatra was there to dedicate the new building. The society editor asked that I go with her. I had to wear a tuxedo. I got to shoot Frank Sinatra from about the third row. Then we went upstairs to the special parties. We ate well and then drove back to Toledo, 120 miles, well after midnight, and got the prints out. It gave me a bit of overtime and, you know, something different. I figured the paper would get me for it. This was on a Saturday night. The following Wednesday and Thursday, they got me. I had just come on in the afternoon, and they said they had a story on a sewer in west Toledo. They want me to go. So there you have it. From the top of society to the sewers.

Really, the new sewer was probably more fun and challenging. We traveled underground for about a mile and a half inside the sewer. It was cool until we got to the area where they were pouring concrete, at the advancing end. Then the temperature went up to between 108 and 112 degrees, from the reaction of the setting concrete. The total lighting I had to work with was a string of clear, naked lightbulbs, about 100 watts each. I would go into the work area to take a picture and the camera would get hot. When I would walk back out of the work area, the cool moist air would condense moisture all over my camera. I carry towels in my bag most of the time. They were soaked by the time I was done, from wiping the camera off.

So you see, my job is really varied, and I think I enjoy almost all of it.

What assignments do you dislike, then?

I think when you go and shoot just head shots. I don't dislike it, but it gets to be production work. You go to a wrestling match and shoot head shots of all thirty wrestlers, then come back and print all thirty. This is not photography.

Any advice to young photographers entering the field?

You've got to really enjoy photography. Most of our photographers shoot all the time for themselves when they're not working.

How important is the credit line, the by-line?

I think that if they gave more credit lines, more photographers' work would improve. If you have your name stuck on a picture, you want it to be good. I think a by-line does improve the quality. And if you plan to go somewhere else, it can be very important. I think editors see that by-line.

Back to advice to young photographers. Bowling Green State University turns out about 110 to 130 journalistic photographers every year. The instructor in photojournalism, who is a very good friend of mine, says that if he can place eight out of 125 students, he feels that is good. The field is very competitive and very hard to break into.

How do you feel, as a news photographer, about intruding into someone's grief or other sensitive areas?

I suppose to say that a photographer should not cover these areas is to say that the Pulitzer Prizes are all wrong. You have to get your hands dirty once in a while. You can't really say later, "Well, gee, that would have been a good picture." You have to keep shooting. I try to do it without being obnoxious. Sure, people are grief-stricken. I have seen them go out of their heads and attack photographers, simply because the photographer just comes up and sticks a camera in. Sometimes you have to be prepared to do some fast talking. Yet I think this stuff has a right to be covered. If you see the movies today, what's sacred anymore?

Would you go into photojournalism again?

Yes. I wouldn't have as many hangups about plagiarism and copying other work or styles, because you realize that nothing is new in photography. Even though you do it your photographic way, and I do it my photographic way, I feel I can improve on it. The next kid that comes along feels he can improve on it. By each of us doing the same old themes, but trying new angles on them, we are going to improve the field.

Jim
Wallace

The card reads, " 'Design in Nature' photography by Jim Wallace." Mr.
Wallace is a nature photographer. Of that there can be no question. But he
doesn't pursue lions in the veldt, or toucans in the jungle, or even sparrows
in the backyard. He creates fine images of natural things, in superlative
color. He seeks to communicate with his viewer by sensitizing the viewer to
the environment in which we all survive and by which we are all nourished.

His pictures come as much from his mind and soul as from his camera
and darkroom. They are planned and foreseen more than found and captured. Color is a major element in his work. Representing him in this book
with a black and white print does not do justice to his artistry.

Mr. Wallace also has another professional policy that is not practiced by
any other photographer represented here: He sells all his work as limited
editions, directly to the final owner, via outdoor art shows. This puts him in
the forefront of bringing photography, and particularly color photography, as a fine art, to the attention of the general public. And he is succeeding.

When Mr. Wallace isn't traveling, he can be found at home in Niagara
Falls, New York.

What is your background?

I am thirty-two years old. I was born and raised in the Niagara frontier
area. Did my high school and college education locally, and I have been
teaching in this area.

What did you study in college?

I started out in biology and wound up in environmental biology. With my final graduate work, I wound up teaching environmental education for quite a number of years. That's really what triggered the whole photographic process. I didn't own a camera five years ago.

Continue with this. How did you get into it?

Well, I've been into the environmental thing for quite a long time. I've always enjoyed nature and backpacking and all kinds of outdoor things. I used to take a small camera, an Instamatic, and I figured it wasn't worth taking. The things I was seeing just weren't coming out on film. So I picked up a second hand camera and decided to start working with it, and I had some fairly positive feedback from people. I just began, then, pushing things as far as they'd go. After about five years, I've finally reached the point where I can make a living at it. This is my last year of teaching. I'm finishing up in the next couple of weeks. I've got shows planned all over the country. I've been doing shows, pretty much in the summer, and a few shows during the rest of the year, for about the last three years.

How do you arrange your shows? Do you do your own work or do you have a rep?

No. Basically, they are outdoor shows, they are mall shows, they are shows that I hear about, people that hear about me, invite me to some shows, things like that. Basically, it's grapevine. That's the way the entire arts-and-crafts traveling circuit works. That's what I'm involved in right now. I feel it is a very positive way to see what the market is, and to see what people really want. I'm getting incredible feedback from the shows. So it basically tells me whether my work is good or bad. It's been pretty positive.

Are you using any galleries?

I've been kind of soured on galleries. Galleries don't seem to move the photography. About all I've worked with is galleries in the local area, and in Toronto. I haven't had too much luck up there. I've done a few galleries but it hasn't been very successful. I do much better doing the outdoor shows. The overhead is much, much less. I don't have to worry about the gallery percentage, which is high. It's a lot easier if I just do it myself.

What areas have you covered in the shows?

Up to this time, I've done pretty much up into Ontario, I've done all the way across to New Hampshire and Maine. And now I'm going to be doing heavily metropolitan areas—Boston, Chicago, Milwaukee, Baltimore, Philadelphia, D.C., the Florida circuit in the wintertime. Pretty much the areas that are traditionally circuit areas.

Have you considered trying to sell your work in any other way?

As far as working with magazines, posters, calendars, things like that, no. I've considered it and rejected the idea so far.

Why so?

One, it means working with transparency film, and I don't like the quality of transparencies. I'd much rather produce a print from a negative. Basically because I have so much control in the darkroom. Most of the feedback I get is because of the quality of the work I am doing, and the quality itself is largely due to the work in the darkroom. I have so much control over the colors, the work itself as a whole, the philosophical background of it. Everything I do has a very, very basic idea.

Do you want to elaborate on that a little bit?

That goes back, again, to the environmental situation. "Design in Nature" is the theme on which I work. That's basically what my business is called, "Design in Nature." I have always felt that there is a tremendous gap, tremendous split, between man and the environment. That's why I went into environmental education in the first place. I've worked with the kids, tried to familiarize them with the natural world, to get them to just stop and appreciate some of the common things, some of the more natural things around them. Everything has become so synthetic. It's been said many times, but I really firmly believe it, and I'm working with it. The images that I am working with are very simplistic. They've been isolated in many ways, and rather than work from a subject standpoint, I'm working from the qualities within the subject. Personally, I really don't care what the subject is, whether it is a green pepper, or whether it is a leaf, or what it is. Basically, it's the qualities, it's the mood that's part of the whole situation. That's the feedback that I get from people. So I'm accomplishing what I wanted to accomplish. I figure the best way to be sure the public is receiving your message is if they are willing to support you financially. And I find that they are doing very well.

Have you had any formal photographic training of any kind?

None whatsoever. In fact, a lot of people have come and asked me if I would work with them, if I would take on an apprentice. I had a professional photographer who works for a studio in Buffalo come up to me last week. He was very dissatisfied with the technical attitude of commercial photography and wanted to know if I would be willing to take on an apprentice.

You've been totally self-taught then?

Yes. It's all been trial and error. I think, from the results I've had, that it's been easy for me. The work that I've done has been easy for me. The sales have not been easy, because I've been working the last few years trying to convince people that photography is a legitimate art form. But my images have been coming as I wanted them, and they've been progressing. I've never reached a plateau. They just keep moving. I've been very, very happy with it. There's a hell of a lot of hard work involved.

Do you get a more or less general response to your work, and does that response reflect what you feel you were looking for when you made that image or print?

That pretty much goes along with part of my whole philosophy of the work itself. I have avoided any type of specific situation. I have totally avoided, as much as possible, specific areas that can be easily misunderstood or misinterpreted.

You say you've never reached a plateau. Do you expect to?

I know damned well that there is a lot of hard work left. I've planned a very slim budget for the next couple of years. If things keep going like they have been recently, I'll be jumping up and down and doing handstands. I figure there's going to be some good shows and some bad shows, and who knows?

I gather your basic push, then, is the images and the message rather than the money. You want to make a living at it, but money is not the object.

All I really care about is that I have a place where I don't have to worry about being cold, enough food to eat, a reasonable quality of food, and enough gas to get me around, because that's part of it, too. In doing the shows, I get to see the country. I get to see the areas, get back into the areas I really want to. The more areas I get to, the more experiences I have, the more things I see, the wiser I become as far as photography is concerned. And that's what it's all about, really. It's not going to take too much to keep me happy. As long as I can keep the shows going, as long as I can keep the work going. The biggest expense I have, even beyond my mortgage and everything else, is my photographic expenses. Paper, processing. It's more expensive for me to do my own work than for me to have a lab do it. I could never have a color lab do my work for me. They could never balance color to the degree that I want it. All it takes is a slight, slight shift of color to change an entire mood. That basically is what I am dealing with right now. It's incredible, the amount of control you can have in the darkroom, working with color.

I price my printing right in line with the labs, because it's worth every cent, time-wise. People just don't know. Printing a 30 x 40 inch print—that is a long, long process. When you are trying to get that thing down to the critical situation, you're trying to have the ultimate control with that thing, that might be a two or three day job.

What kind of camera equipment do you use?

I'm working with a basic amount of equipment. I use Canon for 35mm, the Mamaya for the 6 x 7 cm format, and the Argus-Swiss for my 4 x 5 work, so I have all three systems.

I find that there is no crossing lines between systems. Ideally, a particular image has to be done in a particular format. For example, my 35mm work is pretty much quick and easy. In a lot of my macro work, a lot of my soft work, I'm not really interested that much in detail. There are so many qualities that I work with. I work with detailed light, everything else. But when I'm just dealing with color forms and color masses, I don't really need the detail. I can use the 35mm and be just as happy. It would be a waste of effort to use anything else, and in many cases I couldn't even get it down. Because I might wind up with an extension four or five feet long with a 4 x 5, and I've got a reasonable extension for my macro work with my 35mm. 6 x 7 is quite versatile. Yet it doesn't fit into the 35mm slot. When I really want detail, I go to the 4 x 5, but the 4 x 5 isn't very quick when you are working in a constantly changing situation.

Do you shoot a lot?

I shoot a lot. I shoot a lot, really. I shoot a whole lot less than I used to though. I know pretty much what I want. I couldn't even begin to describe the mental process in working with the images. The whole idea of preconception is really part of this work. The whole image begins in my mind, and it has to follow the cycle. It has to come around full circle. It has to come back for the same timing. It's like an element in time. I previsualize, I see something in my mind. It might be a color shift from what I presently see. It might be softer. I know what liberties I can take in the darkroom. So I see something, in reality, but my mind sees something in a different way. I'll record that image on film, and that's basically raw material. I run down my proof sheets—I make proof sheets of the whole situation—I study the proof sheets. I usually rip them up within a week or so, cut out the particular pieces I want, cut the negatives, put them in glassine envelopes, and put the proof shot over it. Then I may spend, usually, in the neighborhood of a year examining the images and working with them, trying to decide. It's pretty rare when I get an image in under six months, a final, limited-edition print.

What is your limited edition?

Right now, I am working with twenty. It's a comfortable number to deal with, and the prices I charge make it worthwhile. That's basically how much I feel it is worth.

How do you guarantee these editions?

I cut the negative in half. It's in the envelope and can be checked.

How do you feel about that?

It doesn't bother me at all. It's almost like being a whore, just printing an image out. What's the sense of just printing and printing and printing? Repetition is not conducive to the art form.

Once you have captured the image, have you done what you want to do?

Yes. A few people will have the satisfaction of owning it. I don't know if it really enhances the value of the image, but I don't think that really matters. I think the fact that there is a limited quantity [is satisfying to the owner].

You say that you previsualize. Do you say, "Aha! I've got a great idea for a picture," and do you go look for the subject that will do it?

I have a lot of very broad mental images. I would say that 80 percent of my work comes from [in effect] my own backyard. Because I am familiar with it. I know what is there. I can go back to the same set of mushrooms. I know basically what earth will support what type of life. It's really amazing how consistent nature is. And I know pretty well what the situations are going to be. It's a lot of waiting for the right moment, waiting for the right set of environmental circumstances, to get the feeling that you really want. Again, the whole idea is a feeling, for the people who see my photography. I would like them to get the feeling that they are part of the environment, that the environment does have a direct relationship to them. It's not just something that's set aside. And that, basically, is what man feels. Man feels that environment is here and man is over there. But if they can become involved with it, [that can change]. [Someone's] idea was that you have to see like a tree, you have to actually feel the environment. If I can make people do that, then I'm really happy.

Do you see yourself as an artist or a photographer?

I don't know. I don't know if I'd really want to put a label on it. I suppose in some ways I consider myself an artist and in other ways I consider myself a photographer. I'm an art photographer. I don't think there is any [reasonable] separation of the two. I think there are all kinds of photographers and all kinds of artists. I think one can be the other.

What kind of film do you use?

I work with Kodacolor II. Right now, I'm trying to get Kodak to run me out some 4 x 5 Kodacolor II, because they consider Kodacolor II to be an amateur film. The whole thing is set up on a commercial basis, and for what the commercial photographers want, using strobe lights and all, the Ektacolors are the finest things for them. But they're not at all good for me. I like a film that I can take on a trip and leave in the refrigerator for two or three weeks, and process it when I get home and not have to worry about the latent image. I feel Kodacolor II is fine. I feel it has as good a resolution as any of the professional films. I just don't shoot transparency film. I have no use for it. I'm not doing magazine work. If I try to make prints from it, they are just too dense. I lose at both ends of the scale. A lot of my work is very soft anyway, so it just doesn't work out. And you don't have the control in the darkroom. With a transparency, either you have it or you don't have it. A negative has so much more latitude.

What kind of chemistry do you use?

I'm using Unicolor chemistry, and I do some of my large work in outside labs that use Hunt chemistry. Hunt seems to be pretty good chemistry for low production. I am a low production printer.

You have no outside work done?

None. My premise is 100 percent control. I don't even send the film out. I'm afraid of it coming back wrecked, and there's a lot of work put into the negatives I am using. They are totally unrepeatable. It's not like working in the studio. When I have found the situation that I want, it is probably a one-shot deal. I've gone back, and I've tried to do things at different times and, no matter how similar the situations are, my head's not in the same place as it was the first time, and it just doesn't work out well.

Do you do any black and white?

I'd like to do more black and white. I like color too much. I'm far behind with my color work now. My dream is to eventually find a person who can come in and print for me exclusively. My own personal printer who knows exactly what I want. But basically this is where I am at right now. I couldn't guarantee that I'll be here six months from now. I may decide I like working with transparency film. I may decide I like doing something with more contrast. I try to be continually changing. It seems that my particular ideas run in streams, and then they seem to fade out and new ideas come in. . . . At first I started out doing some very detailed stuff, very crisp. But then I got into some stuff last summer that was extremely soft. I've had a lot of people come by—I've had a lot of *watercolorists* come by—thinking that I was working with watercolors. I'm underprinting and diffusing in the dark-room, and really drawing the light so that it's really soft and very subtle, and it blends right out to a pure white paper, even in a scenic.

Now, just recently, I switched totally. Now I'm working with my 35mm camera almost exclusively. I'm down, I'm shooting the thing wide open, I'm using very, very shallow depth of field. Extreme isolationist-type stuff. I love it. Last year I broke off and started doing what I call my Kitchen series. It's still life. It's fruits and vegetables. Just taking the forms and working with forms and designs.

You don't place any restrictions on yourself.

No. Whatever I feel like doing, I do. And that's what I decided. People told me a long time ago that I could very easily get into a studio and make a living. But I wasn't really looking for a nine-to-five job. There are of course some very creative commercial photographers, but still they are tied down to somebody else. What I'm doing, in essence, is free-lance, in the ulti-mate sense, and if it's not good enough. . . .

I have to know pretty much what people want. I have to know my market and combine that with the images. That's the only compromise I make. I don't have, other than with marketing and doing shows, a whole lot of deadlines. I'm not tied to the city, I'm not tied to the market. My market is so far away and so widespread that it doesn't make any difference whether I live in the city or the country. I can live where I want to.

When I'm traveling, trying to get in tune with the images is a *really* traumatic experience. Last summer, we went out west and did Glacier in Montana and then went up through Alberta and British Columbia. I had very, very big images in mind. And all of a sudden nothing was working. I spent two solid days, sixteen to eighteen hours each, just trying to get an idea of what was there and what was to be attacked. We did everything. We camped in the information booth there and talked to as many people as we possibly could. We drove around and stopped at the various ranger stations and asked them all kinds of questions. Told them basically what I was doing, what I was interested in, and found out what kind of ideas they had. We picked up a bunch of kids going through Glacier and told them, "I'm only picking you up on the terms that you tell me something. I need some information. Basically this is what I want to do. Give me some ideas, give me some good areas. Cut down on my walking time." It really worked out, but it was two days of hell. I didn't know what I was doing.

Mental hell?

Yes. I could hardly sleep. I find that happens. I find that happens as I move into different areas. But once I become more familiar with the area. . . . I can't just burn the film. I have to have a definite idea of what's happening.

It's a much different approach than almost any I have been acquainted with. You don't seem to work with an eye for grabbing a chunk out of time when you just see it. You're tuned in from a different direction, some place . . . ahead of time. I'm trying to understand it.

My total picture, my total image, is pretty much developed before I shoot.

You consider photography an art form?

I approach it strictly as a fine art. My only goal in my work is to communicate a particular feeling to people, and allow them enough freedom to create their own experiences. I feel that is basically what the whole idea of fine art is all about. But as far as photography being accepted as a fine art form, that's really something that's just beginning to open up. I remember when I first started doing the shows, I was asked questions like, "What's photography doing in an art show?" It kind of bothered me at the time, but I don't hear it that much anymore because people have seen enough photography by now. But people just didn't want to accept it because Kodak had set it up as the "everyman's" thing to do. Everybody could take a picture. I still hear things like, "Well, Martha, I'll have to go home and get that camera out and try and do some of this stuff." Some of my best customers are amateur photographers, because they know what's basically involved in it.

But it's really picked up. It's snowballed. It's like a wave moving forward. It's becoming more and more accepted as people understand it more. I think there was a tremendous amount of ignorance about photography until just recently. Especially color photography. Black and white has been accepted to some extent. Color photography is just really now becoming accepted as an art form. It seems to build. Basically, it is most accepted around metropolitan areas today. I did a tour last year through New Hampshire and Maine. They tried to throw me out of the shows. I knew that they didn't want photography before I went. But I went up and pushed it anyhow. And I got into the shows and I did fairly well. That was part of the problem. I did as well as the watercolorists and the oil people. I got a letter this year saying that due to my interaction, photography is now considered part of the shows.

People are afraid to think for themselves a lot of times. They wait for some biggies to say that it's okay. Now that some very prominent galleries are starting to show photography, it is becoming acceptable.

INDEX